Student Prep Book
Jean Nankivell

SIXTH EDITION

English For Careers

BUSINESS, PROFESSIONAL, AND TECHNICAL

Leila R. Smith
Margaret Taylor

PRENTICE HALL, UPPER SADDLE RIVER, NEW JERSEY 07458

Production Supervisor: *Barbara Cassel*
Director of Production: *Bruce Johnson*
Publisher: *Greg Burnell*
Production Manager: *Ed O'Dougherty*
Text Production Editor: *Kathryn Kasturas*

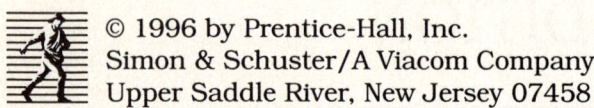
© 1996 by Prentice-Hall, Inc.
Simon & Schuster/A Viacom Company
Upper Saddle River, New Jersey 07458

All rights reserved. No part of this book may be reproduced,
in any form or by any means, without permission in writing from the publisher.

Printed in the United States of America
10 9 8 7 6 5 4 3 2 1

ISBN: 0-13-368093-2

Prentice-Hall International (UK) Limited, *London*
Prentice-Hall of Australia Pty. Limited, *Sydney*
Prentice-Hall Canada Inc., *Toronto*
Prentice-Hall Hispanoamericana, S.A., *Mexico*
Prentice-Hall of India Private Limited, *New Delhi*
Prentice-Hall of Japan, Inc., *Tokyo*
Simon & Schuster Asia Pte. Ltd., *Singapore*

CONTENTS

Chapter 1   TOOLS OF THE TRADE (Parts of Speech)   **1**

Chapter 2   SECRET LIFE OF A SENTENCE REVEALED (Fragments, Run-Ons, Comma Splices)   **10**

Chapter 3   AIN'T IS IN THE DICTIONARY (Dictionary Use)   **17**

Chapter 4   APPLES, TIGERS, AND SWAHILI (Plurals; Compound, Proper, and Biased Nouns)   **21**

Chapter 5   BE KIND TO THE SUBSTITUTE WEEK (Pronouns)   **28**

Chapter 6   LOOKING FOR THE ACTION? (Then Find the Verbs!)   **34**

Chapter 7   WORDS THAT DESCRIBE (Adjectives and Adverbs)   **43**

Chapter 8   THE TAMING OF THE APOSTROPHE   **49**

Chapter 9   THE PAUSE THAT REFRESHES (Commas)   **52**

Chapter 10   PUNCTUATION POTPOURRI (. ? ; : " - ' -- ___)   **61**

Chapter 11   A BUSINESS DICTIONARY (Dictionary of business terms—Spell, Define, Pronounce)   **68**

Chapter 12   WEATHER OR KNOT (Homonyms, Prepositions, Pronunciation)   **74**

Chapter 13   SENTENCE POWER (Conciseness, Smoothness, Parallel Construction, Misplaced Modifiers, Vague Pronouns, Active/Passive Voice, Dangling Verbs)   **80**

Chapter 14   SINCERELY YOURS (Business Letters)   **85**

               ANSWERS TO DRILLS   **87**

CHAPTER 1
TOOLS OF THE TRADE

REPLAY DRILL 1-A

Underline the nouns in the following sentences. The number of nouns in each sentence is in parentheses at the end of each sentence.

Example

The <u>secretary</u> greeted each <u>visitor</u> who entered the <u>building</u>.

1. Shenita handed Mark his textbook. (3)

2. Some students drive over twenty miles to school each day. (4)

3. The assignments were due in two weeks. (2)

4. The syllabi contain all the information for each subject. (3)

5. Tina and Rose sent in their applications for a student loan. (4)

6. Will was embarrassed when his stomach growled during math class. (3)

7. Only five errors are allowed on the typing timings. (2)

8. The instructor announced the examination schedule for next week. (3)

9. Larry rearranged the textbooks, notebooks, and papers in his backpack. (5)

10. The classroom contained twenty computers and five printers. (3)

REPLAY DRILL 1-B

Underline the pronouns in the following sentences. The number of pronouns in each sentence is in parentheses at the end of each sentence.

Example

<u>We</u> gave <u>them</u> directions to the party. (2)

1. She announced that anyone could attend the seminar. (2)

2. Your insurance will cover his hospital bills. (2)

3. John and I received their application in the mail. (2)

4. Who will accept the award for him?. (2)

5. Something was missing from the top of her bureau. (2)

6. I worked twelve hours on this. (2)

7. Everyone in the audience clapped loudly after their presentation. (2)

8. He tried to unscramble the puzzle, but nothing made sense. (2)

9. You must learn the home keys on the typewriter. (1)

10. Those of you who were absent must turn in your assignments. (4)

11. Whomever you select as chairman will choose the new committee members. (2)

12. The girl curled her hair this morning. (1)

13. The panel members asked the judge for her decision. (1)

14. Somebody in the audience dropped his or her wallet on the floor. (3)

15. Since everyone was anxious to leave, no one heard the teacher give the assignment. (2)

16. The class knew that she had won the contest. (1)

17. I thought the eraser was mine, but Betty said it was hers. (4)

18. We are renting a truck and moving ourselves to our new home. (3)

19. The child sat between his mother and me on the bus. (2)

20. Everything in the store will be discounted at the annual sidewalk sale. (1)

REPLAY DRILL 2

Underline the complete verb in the following sentences. Remember to include any helping verbs as part of the complete verb.

Example

Mesissa <u>was elected</u> to the Activities Board.

1. The Admissions Director <u>welcomed</u> each student.

2. Martha <u>will be attending</u> the orientation program on Monday.

3. Bill <u>was</u> eager to see his new class schedule.

4. The counselor <u>has handed</u> each new student a college catalogue.

5. The admissions office <u>required</u> a high school transcript.

6. Stacey <u>will be</u> a student for the first time in ten years.

7. The butterflies <u>were jumping</u> in Maria's stomach on the first day of class.

8. The professor's friendly smile <u>brightened</u> the student's entire day.

9. The young man's laughter <u>echoed</u> throughout the Student Union.

10. The new students <u>were looking</u> forward to the first day of the semester.

4 Student Prep Book

REPLAY DRILL 3-A

Part One Underline the descriptive adjectives in the following sentences. The number of descriptive adjectives is in parentheses at the end of each sentence.

Example

The <u>pepperoni</u> pizza tasted <u>delicious</u>. (2)

1. The irritating caller harassed the busy receptionist. (2)//
2. The tired and thirsty workmen appreciated the cold lemonade. (3)
3. The noisy water pipes rattled throughout the law offices. (3)
4. The slippery tape slid off the wooden desk. (2)
5. The efficient secretary typed the ten-page report. (2)
6. Mr. Thomas had a magnificent view of the inner harbor from his office window. (3)
7. The elegant executive greeted the new clients with a firm handshake. (3)
8. The pages in that old book are faded and torn. (3)
9. The heavier computer paper jammed the printer. (2)
10. The grouchy administrator needed a fresh cup of brewed coffee. (3)

Part Two Underline the one limiting adjective in each sentence.

Example

The sale brought <u>many</u> new customers to the store.

11. Several people rushed into the classroom as the bell rang.
12. Do you have enough time to complete the test?
13. Twenty-five new students enrolled in the course.
14. Her paper contained no errors.
15. The teacher gave Keith a few ideas for his speech.

Part Three Underline the one pointing adjective and the one article in each of the following sentences.

16. These checks include the Christmas bonus.
17. A special delivery letter arrived this morning.
18. The accounting manager requested that software program.
19. An angry customer returned those broken file cabinets.
20. This reference book has an excellent chapter on economics.

REPLAY DRILL 3-B

Underline the one adverb in the following sentences.

Example

Amy types <u>quickly</u>.

1. Ron <u>finally</u> proposed to Mary.
2. Jonas worked <u>diligently</u> on his homework.
3. The report is due <u>immediately</u>.
4. The new computer is <u>very</u> expensive.
5. Turner worked <u>well</u> with the other employees.
6. Mr. Jones <u>really</u> wanted a raise.
7. Cynthia was an <u>extremely</u> talented singer.
8. Michael <u>almost</u> lost the contract.
9. The secretarial applicant was dressed <u>appropriately</u>.
10. These figures are added <u>accurately</u>.
11. Many products are <u>cheaply</u> manufactured.
12. Mr. Johnson <u>never</u> arrives on time.
13. The clerk was working <u>hard</u> on the filing project.
14. The <u>most</u> outstanding employee of the year received an award.
15. The paper was <u>too</u> messy to read.
16. Her voice is <u>exceptionally</u> loud on the telephone.
17. The computer <u>rapidly</u> produced the results of the survey.
18. John's new haircut is <u>so</u> stylish.
19. Mr. Perkins is <u>not</u> attending the conference.
20. The supervisor demanded his resignation <u>now</u>.

REPLAY DRILL 4

Part One   Underline the conjunctions in the following sentences.

Example

Brenda <u>and</u> Barbara were late for work.

1. Everyone <u>but</u> Andy attended the conference.

2. Shannon left class <u>when</u> the teacher was finished lecturing.

3. They waited under the tree <u>until</u> the rain stopped.

4. Ryan studied hard <u>so that</u> he would pass the test.

5. The supervisor requested <u>that</u> James <u>or</u> Linda stay after work.

6. The couple wanted to go to the movies, <u>but</u> it was too late.

7. The crowd waited in the lobby <u>while</u> the elevator was being repaired.

8. Al <u>and</u> Jeremy hurried to the office <u>since</u> the meeting was about to begin.

9. The employees didn't know <u>if</u> they had received a raise.

10. The instructor praised the students <u>whenever</u> they answered the questions correctly.

Part Two   Underline the prepositional phrases in the following sentences.

Example

Carol went <u>with me</u>.

11. Please put the typewriter <u>on the desk</u>.

12. The secretary put the papers <u>in the folder</u>.

13. The sun broke <u>through the clouds</u>.

14. The flowers were blooming <u>along the path</u>.

15. The store owners lived <u>above the business</u>.

16. The clerk bumped <u>into the file cabinet</u>.

17. Louise moved her car <u>across the street</u>.

18. Everyone <u>except Luther</u> will be going <u>on the business trip</u>.

19. Several people were talking <u>during the lecture</u>.

REPLAY DRILL 5-A

Identify the underlined words as either nouns, verbs, or adjectives.

Example

He signed up to take dance lessons. (adjective)

1. She put her money in the bank.

2. Jim was training to be a bank teller.

3. The store's motto was, "You can bank on us!"

4. In what time zone do you live?

5. I will time the runners.

6. Do you have the time to read this assignment?

7. The baseball game's final score was 7 to 5.

8. Lincoln scored the winning touchdown.

9. The caddie kept the score card during the golf match.

10. The swim coach taught Darla the backstroke.

11. He will swim each morning to keep in shape.

12. The long swim across the lake was exhausting.

13. Martin shops for bargains.

14. The shop manager retired after thirty years.

15. That new shop has good bargains.

16. Mrs. Brown's garden contains over one hundred flowers.

17. The garden market sold fresh vegetables.

18. Mother said she will garden after breakfast.

19. The cashier could not read the amount on the price tag.

20. We must price the furniture at several stores.

REPLAY DRILL 5-B

Part One   Underline the subject in the following sentences.

Example

<u>Mary</u> cooked dinner.

1. The receptionist answered the telephone.
2. Chris won the tennis match.
3. The thirsty children drank all the lemonade.
4. A two-page composition is due each week.
5. Each answer is worth ten points.
6. The lightning hit our maple tree.
7. Her picture was on the cover of the magazine.
8. The beach was full of sunbathers.
9. Mr. Gomez won the data entry award.
10. Summertime seems to fly by.

Part Two   Underline the verb in the following sentences.

11. The audience clapped loudly for the speaker.
12. Mr. Leery announced the new schedules.
13. The policeman handcuffed the prisoner.
14. The ice cream melted in the hot sun.
15. The boys and girls raced to the swing set.
16. Ms. Robinson typed the business report.
17. The crowd cheered after the touchdown.
18. The pizza maker tossed the dough into the air.
19. The magician's trick stunned the audience.
20. The heavy rain flooded the streets.

BONUS DRILL 6

Refer to the business letter in the textbook on page 28 regarding the newly purchased van.

1. In the second sentence of the second paragraph, what part of speech is, <u>However</u>?

2. Underline the dependent clause in this sentence.

3. Underline the independent clause in the third sentence of the paragraph that starts <u>Although</u>.

4. List all of the articles in the last paragraph of the letter._____

5. List all of the verbs, including helping words, in the last paragraph._____

6. List all of the pronouns in the last paragraph._____

7. What part of speech joins or connects two words or groups of words?_____

8. Which part of speech tells something about a noun or pronoun?_____

9. Which part of speech expresses action or being?_____

10. What names something, somebody, or someplace?_____

CHAPTER 2
SECRET LIFE OF A SENTENCE REVEALED

REPLAY DRILL 7

Decide if the following word groups are complete sentences (C) or if they are fragments (incomplete thoughts) (F).

Example

When the bell rang for class F

1. The payroll clerk computed the salaries

2. While the payroll clerk computed the salaries

3. Provided you can begin the job Monday

4. You can begin the job on Monday

5. The instructor's lecture lasted the whole hour

6. Since the instructor's lecture lasted the whole hour

7. The boss handed George his paycheck

8. Unless the boss handed George his paycheck

9. The employees left the office at 5 o'colck.

10. After the employees left the office at 5 o'clock

11. As Mr. Harrison accepted the award

12. Mr. Harrison accepted the award

13. The secretary typed all the reports in two hours

14. Although the secretary typed all the reports in two hours

15. Because Mr. Schaffer handed in his resignation

16. Mr. Schaffer handed in his resignation

17. All the class members passed the final exam

18. Until all the class members passed the final exam

19. Marsha spoke with the new professor

20. If Marsha spoke with the new professor

REPLAY DRILL 8

Decide if the following word groups are complete sentences (C) or if they are fragments (incomplete thoughts) (F).

Example

Mr. Johnson who is our manager (F)

1. The receptionist, who was away last week
2. The receptionist returning to work today
3. The receptionist returned to work today
4. The board meeting, which will be held on Friday
5. The board meeting will be held on Friday
6. The board meeting being held on Friday
7. The education director, who is Mr. Bryant
8. The education director is Mr. Bryant
9. Norfolk, being a large U.S. Navy port
10. Norfolk, which is a large U.S. Navy port
11. Norfolk is a large U.S. Navy port
12. The graduate who received her diploma
13. The graduate, while receiving her diploma
14. The graduate received her diploma
15. Mr. Mathews, while speaking to the business students
16. Mr. Mathews is speaking to the business students
17. Mr. Mathews, speaking to the business students
18. Betsy Ross's house, which is in Philadelphia
19. Betsy Ross's house, being in Philadelphia
20. Betsy Ross's house is in Philadelphia.

REPLAY DRILL 9

Identify the following word groups as either a complete sentence (C), a comma splice (CS), or a run-on (R).

Example

Mom baked some cookies they tasted delicious (R)

1. The secretary handed the report to the supervisor, he read it quickly
2. When the secretary handed the report to the supervisor, he read it quickly
3. The secretary handed the report to the supervisor he read it quickly
4. While the lawyer prepared the case, her assistant checked the reference sheets
5. The lawyer prepared the case her assistant checked the reference sheets
6. The lawyer prepared the case, her assistant checked the reference sheets
7. The corporation expanded its holding; it now oversees $2 billion a year.
8. Since the corporation expanded its holdings, it now oversees $2 billion a year
9. The corporation expanded its holdings, it now oversees $2 billion a year
10. The corporation expanded its holdings it now oversees $2 billion a year
11. The reporter wrote the award-winning story, it was published in over two hundred newspapers
12. The reporter wrote the award-winning story; it was published in over two hundred newspapers
13. The reporter wrote the award-winning story it was published in over two hundred newspapers
14. The company jet flew to London, all the major executives were aboard
15. When the company jet flew to London, all the major executives were aboard
16. The company jet flew to London, all the major executives were aboard
17. When the mayor spoke to the council, all the members listened
18. The mayor spoke to the council, all the members listened
19. The mayor spoke to the council all the members listened
20. The mayor spoke to the council; all the members listened

REPLAY DRILL 10-A

Part One   Underline the transition words in the following sentences.

Example

I hurried to work, <u>yet</u> I was still late.

1. Barbara did not study for her test; <u>therefore</u>, she was happy to see the barely passing grade.
2. Ron worked hard to get good grades; <u>for example</u>, he reviewed his class notes every night.
3. Mrs. Williams expected the best from her students; <u>hence</u> they were always prepared in class.
4. Please hand in your homework; <u>then</u> you may begin working on the next assignment.
5. Rose did not hear the alarm; <u>consequently</u>, she was late arriving for English class.
6. Twenty-five percent of the class received an "A"; <u>furthermore</u>, all the students passed the test.
7. Please sign in if you are late; <u>otherwise</u>, you will be marked absent.
8. Laura lost her wallet in class; <u>however</u>, someone turned it in to the office.
9. The instructor handed out the course outline; <u>in fact</u>, she explained every assignment.
10. The copy machine broke down; <u>nevertheless</u>, the teacher had the test ready for class.
11. Each student needs to rent a locker in the Student Union Building; <u>also</u>, he or she must purchase a new lock.
12. The graduation ceremony is Saturday night; <u>in addition</u>, the practice will be Thursday morning.
13. The instructor gave a reading assignment; <u>moreover</u>, she also assigned a three-page composition.
14. Stephanie had completed the assignment at home, <u>thus</u> she had time to work on the next assignment in class.
15. The director introduced the speaker; <u>that is</u>, he gave a summary of the speaker's qualifications.

Part Two   Underline the conjunction that joins the independent clauses in the following sentences.

Example

Edna typed the report, <u>and</u> she left it on Mr. Brown's desk.

16. Tondra decided to attend business college, <u>for</u> she wanted to increase her job skills.
17. Greg found his wallet, <u>but</u> his money was missing.
18. The sun is shining, <u>yet</u> the rain is beginning to pour down.
19. You cannot pay by check <u>nor</u> can you charge the purchase to your account.
20. Richard will speak on Thursday <u>or</u> he will send a replacement

REPLAY DRILL 10-B

Decide if the following word groups are a complete sentence (C), a run-on (R), or a comma-splice (CS).

Example

Since Teresa had a 4.0 average, she was an honor graduate. (C)

1. Mark graduated in June he has had several job offers

2. Since Mark graduated in June, he has had several job offers

3. Mark graduated in June, he has had several job offers

4. The Graduate Assistant gave the instructions, she then passed out the test

5. The Graduate Assistant gave the instructions she then passed out the test

6. The Graduate Assistant gave the instructions before she passed out the test

7. The Graduate Assistant gave the instructions; she then passed out the test

8. The information is inaccurate, the report cannot be completed

9. The information is inaccurate; the report cannot be completed

10. The information is inaccurate the report cannot be completed

11. If the information is inaccurate, the report cannot be completed

12. Anthony was called for a job interview, his resumé impressed the employer

13. Anthony was called for a job interview because his resumé impressed the employer

14. Anthony was called for a job interview his resumé impressed the employer

15. Bernice felt her life was going nowhere, she enrolled in a business college

16. Bernice felt her life was going nowhere; she then enrolled in a business college

17. Bernice felt her life was going nowhere until she enrolled in a business college

18. As if he understood the language, Danny listened to the man speak Spanish

19. Danny listened to the man speak Spanish, he understood the language

20. Danny listened to the man speak Spanish as though he understood the language

REPLAY DRILL 11

Underline the dependent clause in each sentence.

1. <u>After the workers finished the project</u>, they all received bonuses.

2. The sun was shining brightly <u>until the clouds moved in</u>.

3. <u>Because the biscuits were hard</u>, the family refused to eat them.

4. <u>Since Susan left town</u>, there is not a great swimmer on the team.

5. <u>When salesmen are successful</u>, the company reaches it's goal.

6. <u>Although we had a wet spring</u>, the water table is still low.

7. Esther and David are planning to get married soon <u>even though they have no money</u>.

8. John F. Kennedy delivered many great speeches <u>when he was president</u>.

9. <u>Even though his supervisor gave clear directions</u>, Mark still made several mistakes on his report.

10. <u>Since wrong answers will be subtracted from the total number of correct responses</u>, do not guess.

BONUS DRILL 12

Make one of the clauses a dependent one and connect it to an independent one.

1. John is an excellent student. John gets good grades.

2. The manager of the store trains the employees very well. The store has the highest sales in the district.

3. The short story was very dramatic. The students in the English Composition class responded enthusiastically.

4. Modern psychologists do not all agree with Freud's theories. Freud focused on biological and sexual drives.

5. Senator Dole attacked the moral standards of modern music. The public has mixed views on the subject.

6. Jeff Smith is television's *Frugal Gourmet*. Last week he prepared three different chicken dishes.

7. The Accounting Department will issue new expense forms this week. Many people were confused on how to tabulate mileage reports.

8. The American Indians were unfairly presented in films of the forties and fifties. Very few sympathetic portrayals of Native Americans were presented.

9. I cannot pay my car payment this month. Our checks are late coming from the home office.

10. Bob and Art are sitting on the fence. Susan and Janet are running down the hill.

CHAPTER 3
AIN'T IS IN THE DICTIONARY

REPLAY DRILL 13

Part One   Use your dictionary to discover the etymology of the following words:

1. ruthless
2. assassin
3. chauvinistic
4. odyssey
5. chaos
6. tantalize
7. antebellum
8. a la mode
9. charlatan
10. polyglot

Part Two   Use your dictionary to find the meaning of the following words:

11. embryology
12. geology
13. seismologist
14. quark
15. hieroglyphics
16. egocentric
17. neurosis
18. agoraphobia
19. anthropology
20. demographics

REPLAY DRILL 14

Rewrite the misspelled words.

1. absense　　　_____
2. accurasy　　_____
3. analyse　　　_____
4. attendence　_____
5. britian　　　_____
6. cemetary　　_____
7. changable　 _____
8. changeing　 _____
9. comeing　　 _____
10. defered　　_____
11. dineing　　_____
12. excelince　_____
13. existance　_____
14. fourty　　　_____
15. grammer　　_____
16. grievious　_____
17. inevitable _____
18. lonliness　_____
19. ninty　　　_____
20. omited　　　_____

REPLAY DRILL 15

Write the number of syllables in each word.   Use your dictionary.   Show where the syllables are divided.

1. September   _____
2. wonderful   _____
3. merriment   _____
4. methodology   _____
5. totality   _____

Parts of Speech   Write the part or parts of speech for each word.   Use your dictionary.

6. motor   _____
7. metal   _____
8. facility   _____
9. grandeur   _____
10. make   _____

Pronunciation   Write the preferred pronunciation for each word. Use your dictionary.

11. maudlin   _____
12. education   _____
13. literature   _____
14. spastic   _____
15. balloon   _____

Origin   Use your dictionary to find the language or languages of derivation.

16. fanatic   _____
17. syllogism   _____
18. phonetic   _____
19. oration   _____
20. milieu   _____

BONUS DRILL 16

Use your dictionary to determine the meaning of the following:

1. SONAR _____
2. RADAR _____
3. CD ROM _____
4. VCR _____
5. SCUBA _____

Find the meaning of the following terms.

6. aesthetic _____
7. tautologies _____
8. tenuous _____
9. ponder _____
10. scrutinize _____
11. proliferation _____
12. undulate _____
13. astronomical _____
14. lugubrious _____
15. disconcerted _____

Find the language of origin of each of the following words.

16. kinetic _____
17. erudite _____
18. flamboyant _____
19. guillotine _____
20. pianoforte _____

CHAPTER 4
APPLES, TIGERS, AND SWAHILI

REPLAY DRILL 17

Make the following singular nouns plural.

Example

writer   writers

SINGULAR	**PLURAL**
1. baby	_____
2. alloy	_____
3. daisy	_____
4. play	_____
5. rally	_____
6. country	_____
7. church	_____
8. tax	_____
9. wish	_____
10. glass	_____
11. veto	_____
12. echo	_____
13. radio	_____
14. alto	_____
15. leaf	_____
16. roof	_____
17. shelf	_____
18. wife	_____
19. chief	_____
20. dwarf	_____

REPLAY DRILL 18-A

Part One Write the plural of the following nouns. Use a dictionary if needed. If two plurals are acceptable, write both.

Example

basis   bases

SINGULAR	PLURAL
1. thesis	_____
2. bacterium	_____
3. analysis	_____
4. stimulus	_____
5. alga	_____
6. genus	_____
7. hypothesis	_____
8. curriculum	_____
9. memorandum	_____
10. fungus	_____
11. antenna	_____
12. appendix	_____
13. syllabus	_____
14. crisis	_____

Part Two Decide if the following words are singular (S) or plural (P).

Example

fungi   P

15. data _____

16. crisis _____

17. media _____

18. alumni _____

19. algae _____

20. bacterium _____

REPLAY DRILL 18-B

Write S or P to indicate if the following nouns are usually singular or plural.

Example

trousers				P

1. economics			_____
2. statistics			_____
3. news				_____
4. goods				_____
5. thanks				_____
6. scissors			_____
7. civics				_____
8. measles			_____
9. proceeds			_____
10. mathematics		_____

REPLAY DRILL 19-A

Write the plurals of the following proper nouns.

Example

Anderson   Andersons

1. Bush				_____
2. Kelly				_____
3. Jones				_____
4. Hartman			_____
5. James				_____
6. Marie				_____
7. Amy				_____
8. Williams			_____
9. Booth				_____
10. Lois				_____

REPLAY DRILL 19-B

Part One Write the plural form of the following compound nouns.

Example

police chief   police chiefs

SINGULAR	PLURAL
1. get-together	_____
2. post office	_____
3. runner-up	_____
4. cupful	_____
5. son-in-law	_____
6. tapedeck	_____
7. photocopy	_____
8. hand-me-down	_____
9. middleman	_____
10. letter of credit	_____

Part Two Underline any nouns in the following sentences that should be capitalized.

Example

On our vacation we went to England.

11. Ann is studying german and accounting.

12. The building will be closed during the christmas holidays

13. My father retired from united airlines

14. The new schedule will begin on April 1.

15. A letter of reference was signed by commander John Enrico.

16. Your application will be sent to our personnel department.

17. Marvin will be taking statistics 101 next fall.

18. He signed the letter—John L. Smith, purchasing agent.

19. After high school he drove from california to the east coast.

20. John F. Kennedy was the youngest man elected president of the United States.

REPLAY DRILL 20

Underline the biased word in each sentence. Write a more acceptable form for that word.

Example

The <u>salesgirl</u> helped me.   salesperson

1. The fireman received an award for saving the child's life.

2. The lady doctor removed my stitches.

3. Marla's daughter is training to be a stewardess.

4. The girls in the office went to lunch.

5. Danielle Steel is a well-known authoress.

6. The cameraman filmed the protest outside the hospital.

7. The new woman manager spoke to all the employees.

8. The directress of the pageant introduced the contestants.

9. The policeman directed traffic during the power outage.

10. Most women libbers use Ms. in front of a woman's name.

11. That lady lawyer gave an excellent closing argument.

12. The mailman delivered the package to the wrong address.

13. Herbert went to business college for training as a male secretary.

14. The seminary graduated over two hundred clergymen.

15. That diamond is not genuine; it is manmade.

16. The managers and their wives attended the annual banquet.

17. President Bush's spokesman reported to the media.

18. Amy is a fellow worker of mine.

19. Who is the new weatherman on Channel 12?

20. Several workmen went through the picket lines.

REPLAY DRILL 21   VOCABULARY

Correct any misspellings.

1. The little boy found the chocolate frosting to be irresistable. _____

2. Susan's mother bought her a new box of stationary for her birthday. _____

3. The three ladies in the art class enjoyed creating a statute. _____

4. Several new employees will recieve a bonus this year. _____

5. The seven sorority sisters will recomend Mary for initiation. _____

6. Hundreds of people will be picnicing in the park on the Fourth of July. _____

Use your dictionary to find the correct pronunciation. Write it on the line.

7. Susan likes most Italian food except squid. _____

8. The young lovers sought a romantic setting for their rendezvous. _____

9. It is necessary to ascertain the needs of the corporation before embarking on a restructuring plan. _____

10. College students are often interested in playing medieval games such as jousting. _____

11. Complex carbohydrates are an important part of a diet. _____

12. The ferocious animal frightened all of the children on the playground. _____

Use your dictionary to find the meaning of the underlined word.

13. The Shawnees were indigenous to the area.

14. None of us gave credence to the inflammatory ideas of the speaker.

15. Ralph speaks in a Southern Mountain dialect.

16. The anthropologists have made a thorough study of the socioeconomic conditions of this region.

17. Old habits are often ingrained in people.

18. Stereotyping is very common in most social groups.

19. Police brandishing batons finally quelled the riot.

BONUS DRILL 22   PLURALS

Write the plural for each of the following words:

	SINGULAR	PLURAL
1.	medium	_____
2.	cactus	_____
3.	attorney	_____
4.	party	_____
5.	deer	_____
6.	sheep	_____
7.	IRA	_____
8.	child	_____
9.	appendix	_____
10.	bacterium	_____
11.	alumna, alumnus	_____
12.	tooth	_____
13.	alga	_____
14.	series	_____
15.	species	_____
16.	basis	_____
17.	life	_____
18.	calf	_____
19.	hoof	_____
20.	knife	_____

CHAPTER 5
BE KIND TO THE SUBSTITUTE WEEK

REPLAY DRILL 23

Underline the correct pronoun for each sentence.

Example

Please give (I, <u>me</u>) your answer.

1. Bob and (I, me) went to the movies.
2. Give (we, us) the new course outlines.
3. (They, Them) worked hard to complete their assignments.
4. Please pass the test papers to (I, me).
5. (We, Us) teachers are looking forward to vacation.
6. The secretary handed (he, him) the messages.
7. It was (they, them) who were late for class.
8. Bring your baked goods to (we, us) on Saturday morning.
9. Give your answer to (I, me) by this afternoon.
10. (He, Him) will be attending the conference in Atlanta.
11. Mr. Johnson presented the award to (she, her).
12. John sat behind (we, us) at the football game.
13. It was (she, her) who answered the telephone.
14. Jerry sat between George and (I, me) on the bus.
15. The speakers will be Mr. Benjamen and (I, me).
16. The teacher introduced Tracey as well as (I, me) to the class.
17. Everyone stayed after class except Holly and (she, her).
18. (We, Us) graduates will proceed down the aisle when the music begins.
19. The ballots were given out to (we, us) students during first period class.
20. (He, Him) left class before the bell rang.

REPLAY DRILL 24

Part One   Select the correct pronoun to complete the following sentences.

Example

John gave (hisself, <u>himself</u>) a raise.

1. The manager and (he, himself) waited for the paychecks to arrive from the Payroll Department.

2. No one works harder in class than Michael and (she, her).

3. The student council members (themselves, theirselves) made all the food for the bake sale.

4. She arrived in class earlier than (he, him).

5. Please hand the video tape to (me, myself).

6. Barry is just as good a student as (he. him).

7. The other workers left earlier than (I, myself).

8. The barber gave (hisself, himself) a haircut.

9. The committee members (theirselves, themselves) decided to have another meeting in two weeks.

10. We (ourselves, ourself) may try to learn WordPerfect.

Part Two   In the following ten sentences, five contain an error in pronoun usage and five are correct. Correct the error in the sentences which are incorrect, and write C for the sentences which are correct.

11. The author himself autographed the novel.

12. Salinda does not type as fast as myself.

13. Mr. Cone has spoken to the trainees more often than him.

14. I myself worked till the project was completed.

15. The executives may be finding theirselves working overtime this weekend.

16. John hisself was granted a leave of absence from the office.

17. No other student completed the test as quickly as she.

18. It was himself who welcomed us to the conference.

19. Bertina hurt herself during the fire drill.

20. Ann knows her legal terminology better than I.

REPLAY DRILL 25

Underline the correct possessive pronoun in each sentence.

Example

The house is (<u>theirs</u>, there's).

1. The dog buried (its, it's) bone in the backyard.

2. Do you know (whose, who's) book is on the desk?

3. Is (you're, your) mother coming to graduation?

4. (No ones, No one's) project received a grade lower than a "B."

5. Is (yours, your's) the one that has been graded already?

6. (Whose, Who's) going to attend the seminar this afternoon?

7. Almost (everyones, everyone's) job was threatened by the strike.

8. (Their, They're) going with us to the retreat.

9. The encyclopedia is (mines, mine).

10. The newly renovated building on Third Street is (our's, ours).

11. (Its, It's) too late to begin the project now.

12. (Who's Whose) working overtime tonight?

13. If (you're, your) running out of paper, you can use some of mine.

14. (Somebodys, Somebody's) child was crying in the lobby.

15. I hope (your's, yours) is the one selected by the judge.

16. Are you the one (whose, who's) car is doubleparked?

17. Is this (anyone's anyones) jacket under the desk?

18. We will be going to (they're, their) house after the show is over.

19. (My, Mine) children will be in high school next fall.

20. The cat knocked over (it's, its) water bowl.

REPLAY DRILL 26

Select either who or whom to complete each of the following sentences.

Example

The man (who, <u>whom</u>) you just met is my father.

1. Mr. Brooks, (who, whom) is a data entry clerk, received a promotion.

2. Do you know (who, whom) is working overtime?

3. The man (who, whom) the police arrested stole Frank's car.

4. Give the extra food to (whoever, whomever) can use it.

5. Mr. Holley, (who, whom) was elected mayor last week, is also my dentist.

6. (Who, Whom) will you ask to speak to the class?

7. Mr. Harris, (who, whom) I mentioned in my letter, will be arriving next week.

8. The young man, (who, whom) is getting married today, works in Richard's office.

9. The contest winner, (who, whom) will be chosen today, will win a trip to Europe.

10. (Who, Whom) spoke to Mr. Anderson before he left?

11. The baseball manager, (who, whom) the umpire threw out of the game, complained to the team.

12. Give the receipt to (whoever, whomever) paid for the package.

13. The new word processor, (who, whom) was just hired, will start next week.

14. The new city manager, (who, whom) no one has met, will be in the office this afternoon.

15. He is the applicant (who, whom), I am sure, you will want to meet.

16. (Whoever, Whomever) signs up first will be given the opportunity to go to the conference.

17. I am the teacher (who, whom) will be teaching the career development class next quarter.

18. (Whoever, Whomever) you choose for the position should have good computer skills.

19. I wonder (who, whom) will do my work while I am on vacation.

20. The woman (who, whom) I met on the bus is Theresa's mother.

REPLAY DRILL 27

Select the correct form of the pronoun in the following sentences.

Example

(<u>Anything</u>, Any thing) you purchase is 30 percent off.

1. (Everyone, Every one) of the students needed more time to finish the test.
2. (Someone, Some one) left his notebook in class.
3. Do you know if (anybody, any body) is planning on going to the picnic?
4. The teacher asked if (somebody, some body) would carry the textbooks to the office.
5. (Anyone, Any one) of the students' essays could be published in the literary magazine.
6. (Everything, Every thing) seems to be going wrong today.
7. The police could find (nobody, no body) who had witnessed the crime.
8. (Everyone, Every one) in the class applauded after Barbara finished her speech.
9. (Something, Some thing) made a loud crashing noise in the hall during class.
10. (Anything, Any thing) you plan for the conference will be fine with me.
11. Few of the students had (his, their) dictionaries with them.
12. Each of the teachers assigned (her, their) classes a project today.
13. Everyone in the cast gave (his their) best performance.
14. Many of the customers complained about (his, their) purchases.
15. Everybody gave (his, their) best effort to get the job done.
16. Several speakers complimented (his, their) audiences.
17. Anybody can still add (his or her, their) name to the list.
18. Someone must volunteer (his or her, their) name to the list.
19. Both my sons lost (his, their) keys on the same day.
20. Students did not raise (his or her, their) hands to answer the question.

BONUS DRILL 28

Select either its or their to complete each of the following sentences.

1. The class gave (its, their) gift to the college building fund.
2. Each group has (its, their) own type of music.
3. The team celebrated (its, their) first victory.
4. The herd of bison thundered (its, their) way across the plain.
5. The orchestra will play (its, their) first performance on Sunday.
6. The band had to change (its, their) uniforms after the game because of the muddy field.
7. The faculty voted (its, their) attempt for representation of the employees.
8. The union won (its, their) attempt for representation of the employees.
9. The counseling staff voted to endorse (its, their) president's position.
10. The jury pondered (its, their) verdict a long time before announcing it to the judge.

Write a list of ten collective nouns.

11. _____
12. _____
13. _____
14. _____
15. _____
16. _____
17. _____
18. _____
19. _____
20. _____

CHAPTER 6
LOOKING FOR THE ACTION?

REPLAY DRILL 29

Underline the verbs in the following sentences. Then identify the tense of the verb as either present, in progress, past, or future.

Example

Mike is helping this son with his homework.   in progress

1. Dawn jogs to class every morning.

2. Frankie should sing in the concert on Saturday.

3. The baby cries when her mother leaves the room.

4. The audience laughed at the comedian's jokes.

5. Pamela is marrying her childhood sweetheart.

6. We will fly to Orlando next Wednesday.

7. During the week, Brian stays with his uncle.

8. Harry and his wife have been seeing a counselor for several months.

9. The children wanted their parents to buy a new car.

10. The contractor will paint the walls this afternoon.

11. Anthony is typing 50 words per minute.

12. Mark needs a new suit for his interview.

13. Laverne is looking for the bandages in the closet.

14. The band marched during the halftime show.

15. The out-of-stock items will arrive in two weeks.

16. The finance committee recommended a five percent raise for all employees.

17. Christy gained ten pounds on her vacation.

18. John is considering transferring jobs.

19. The teacher will talk with me after class.

20. The ivy climbs up the backyard fence.

REPLAY DRILL 30

Select the correct tense of the verbs in the following sentences.

Example

Jack (wears, <u>wore</u>) a new suit yesterday.

1. Barney has (took, taken) several courses in accounting.

2. The Viet Nam Memorial (stands, stood) as a tribute to all who served in the war.

3. The judge has (spoke, spoken) to our law class twice.

4. We have (saw, seen) the view from the top of the Empire State Building.

5. The couple (ran, run) to catch the bus at the corner.

6. The sun (rises, rose) this morning at 5:45 a.m.

7. The doorbell (rang, rung) several times before Mr. Johnson came to the door.

8. The team has (went, gone) to the playoffs each year.

9. The manager (give, gave) each player a pep talk before the game.

10. Our supervisor (flew, flown) to the corporate headquarters in California.

11. Greg has (ate, eaten) pizza for dinner each night this week.

12. During the party the guest (drank, drunk) a toast to the bride and groom.

13. Mr. Stanko (does, did) the payroll checks each Thursday.

14. When Tiffany enrolled in school, she (chose, chosen) the medical assistant program.

15. That man has (broke, broken) every rule in the book.

16. The temperature has (began, begun) to get colder.

17. The furniture has (wore, worn) well over the years.

18. The professor (took, taken) a leave of absence from his classes.

19. The telephone had (rang, rung) ten times before the operator picked it up.

20. The children had (drank, drunk) all the lemonade and yelled for more.

REPLAY DRILL 31

Select the correct form of the verb in the following sentences.

Example

Peter (broke, broken) one of the dishes.

1. Mrs. Yearby (wrote, written) a letter to the editor.
2. The burglar had (threw, thrown) the furniture around the room.
3. The choir (sang, sung) three hymns during the service.
4. The passengers on the bus were (shook, shaken) by the near accident.
5. The treasure was (hid, hidden) at the end of the rainbow.
6. The ice (froze, frozen) quickly in the new freezer.
7. Everyone had (forgot, forgotten) what time the program would start.
8. The prices of new homes have (fell, fallen) ten percent in the last year.
9. The artist (drew, drawn) a portrait of the couple for their wedding present.
10. The regional managers had (came, come) to Washington for their annual meeting.
11. The strong wind (blew, blown) the clothes off the line.
12. The fish (bit, bitten) the bait on the line.
13. The author has (wrote, written) several articles against child abuse.
14. The team's owner (threw, thrown) the first ball of the game to the pitcher.
15. We have (sang, sung) that same song fifty times during rehearsal.
16. The coins (sank, sunk) to the bottom of the pond.
17. The usher (shook, shaken) the man who had fallen asleep during the movies.
18. The mothers (hid, hidden) the Easter eggs under the bushes in the backyard.
19. The stock prices (fell, fallen) by the end of the trading session.
20. The children had (drew, drawn) a hopscotch pattern on the sidewalk.

REPLAY DRILL 32

Select the correct form of the verb "to be" in the following sentences.

Example

I (am, is) happy about the promotion.

1. (Is, Are) you going to the meeting tomorrow morning?

2. Marissa (is, be) the new receptionist.

3. The immigrants (were, was) greeted upon their arrival.

4. I (had been, been) to Radio City Music Hall when I visited New York City.

5. We (is, are) waiting for your answer.

6. (Is, Are) anybody going with me?

7. You (is, are) required to sign in when you enter the building after hours.

8. (I'd, I would) like to speak to Mr. Bryant about a salary increase.

9. The baseball team (be going, will be going) to play in Montreal next week.

10. Doctor Swenson (be, will be) speaking at the physicians' conference in Norfolk.

11. The textbook shipment (is, are) expected next week.

12. The teachers (is, are) having help sessions after school.

13. Keith (is, are) making waffles for breakfast.

14. The galleys for the new textbook (is, are) being proofread by the editors.

15. The computer disks (was, were) ordered last week.

16. The copy machine (will be, be) repaired by noon.

17. During the summer the children (have been, been) sleeping later than usual each morning.

18. You (was, were) chosen to represent our class at the conference.

19. The employees (has been, have been) working in the new building for over two years.

20. (We'd, We would) like to nominate Mr. Rodriquez as the employee of the month.

REPLAY DRILL 33

Underline the verb and circle the subject in the following sentences.

Example

The (child) <u>grabbed</u> a cookie.

1. The morning sun rose at 6 a.m.
2. The hungry wolves howled throughout the valley
3. Do you have a completed resume?
4. Gourmet cooking is Martina's favorite hobby.
5. Please answer his question immediately.
6. The daily newspaper is delivered each morning.
7. There are 25 students in the communications class
8. Both mother and son were found safe before nightfall.
9. The job placement director sent Andrew on three job interviews.
10. Did you buy a ticket for the afternoon or evening performance?
11. Across the street from our office is our favorite restaurant.
12. Early sign-ups for Little League will be held next Saturday.
13. Across the countryside word spread about the fire.
14. Mr. Overton, along with his wife, attended the mayors' conference in San Francisco.
15. The toy manufacturer recalled the new product because of sharp edges.
16. The boy and his grandfather strolled through the city park.
17. Advancement courses are taught for all employees on Wednesday evenings.
18. Along the outer banks, residents were warned of the approaching hurricane.
19. In the morning Sidney will learn his test scores.
20. All during August the football team practiced in the hot sun.

REPLAY DRILL 34-A

The following word groups include the subject of a sentence. Is this subject singular or plural? Write S for singular and P for plural.

Example

The little curly-haired child   S

1. Anyone in the building
2. The members of the jury
3. Each accountant in the department
4. Most of the children
5. Most of the money
6. Half of the students
7. One fourth of the students
8. Each mother and child
9. Both ladies
10. Penny nor her son
11. Penny nor her sons
12. The award-winning team
13. None of the musicians
14. Few of the members
15. Neither the teacher nor the director
16. Every person in the audience
17. More of the ingredients
18. Williams, Thomas, and Williams, Inc.
19. One gentleman and three ladies
20. None of the employees' suggestions

REPLAY DRILL 34-B

Select the verb that is correct in the following sentences. Locate the subject. If the subject is singular, your verb should be singular. If the subject is plural, your verb should be plural.

Example

Mrs. Smith (<u>runs</u>, run) every morning before work.

1. Kelly (writes, write) an entry in her diary every night.

2. All the students (want, wants) a good grade on the exam.

3. The doctor and his two patients (arrives, arrive) at the emergency room.

4. Neither Mary nor I (am, are) going to the concert.

5. There (was, were) a house on Birch Street for sale.

6. The supervisor, as well as all the executives, (does, do) the job evaluations each six months.

7. Each of the members (is, are) writing a set of by laws.

8. The baby (cries, cry) whenever she is hungry.

9. The new answering machine (records, record) all our messages.

10. The three pathologists (speaks, speak) to the medical classes each quarter.

11. Many a father and son (is, are) involved in Little League.

12. This is the woman who (talks, talk) during class.

13. Here (is, are) the supplies you need.

14. Either Marlin or his friends (is, are) planning to attend the word processing seminar.

15. The herd of horses (tries, try) to swim across the muddy stream.

16. Their mother, who (is, are) an optometrist, examined me for contact lenses.

17. General Electric Corporation (is, are) opening an airplane engine manufacturing plant near my home.

18. Several groups (was, were) touring the monument when the lightning struck.

19. Hartman Industries (has, have) a good profit sharing plan for the employees.

20. The lawyer (does, do) want to represent the client in this case.

REPLAY DRILL 35

Select the correct verb in the following sentences.

Example

I wish I (was, <u>were</u>) twenty pounds thinner.

1. If Alice (was, were) my friend, she would try to understand my problem.
2. Mrs. Williams (was, were) the teacher who became the Virginia Teacher of the Year.
3. Greg (was, were) an actor with the Little Theater.
4. When I (was, were) employed at Camtro, Mrs. Perkins (was, were) my supervisor.
5. Carol wishes that she (was, were) an honor student.
6. If I (was, were) you, I would tell Frances how you feel.
7. Jackie (was, were) a PTA volunteer for the elementary school.
8. The man ran as though he (was, were) a fugitive.
9. Danny wishes he (was, were) the man who was hired.
10. When Richard (was, were) working at night, he slept during the day.
11. If my mother (was, were) the cook, this food would taste better.
12. Dickie Thon (was, were) the player who hit the game-winning homerun.
13. That man (was, were) the one who stole my idea.
14. James wishes he (was, were) on vacation.
15. Marlene dances as though she (was, were) a professional dancer.
16. If I (was, were) you, I would buy that dress.
17. Mr. Smithson (was, were) the man we met at the conference.
18. Mrs. Lawson cooks as though she (was, were) feeding fifty people for dinner.
19. The author wishes he (was, were) finished writing his book.
20. If Patricia (was, were) making more money, she could afford to buy that house.

BONUS DRILL 36

Select the correct word to complete the following sentences.

1. The band (has, have) new uniforms this year.

2. The class (spend, spends) a great deal of time discussing current events.

3. The council (select, selects) a new president from among the members.

4. The committee (has, have) many new responsibilities this season.

5. The team (is, are) ready for Saturday afternoon's opponent.

6. The assembly (greet, greets) each speaker with enthusiasm.

7. Groups in our company (have, has) direct linkage by the use of e-mail.

8. The senate (vote, votes) for its majority leader every two years.

9. The club will take a poll of (its, their) members next Tuesday.

10. The family (scatter, scatters) in every direction when it is time to wash the dishes.

11. The crowd (shout, shouts) its approval when we score.

12. Congress (approve, approves) all budgetary items in committees first.

13. The faculty (decide, decides) all major curriculum matters.

14. The orchestra (play, plays) a thundering crescendo at the end of that movement.

15. Members of the association (pay, pays) annual dues in January.

CHAPTER 7
WORDS THAT DESCRIBE

English for Careers

REPLAY DRILL 37

Select the correct word to complete the following sentences.

Example

Charles gave (them, <u>those</u>) children a ride home.

1. Margaret wanted to buy (this, these) kind of material.
2. Margaret wanted to buy (this, these) kinds of material.
3. The children's mother wanted (them, those) to have a good time.
4. (Them, Here) are my parents.
5. (That, Those) woman is my supervisor.
6. (Them, Those) actors are performing in the program tonight.
7. The repairman fixed (that, those) computers.
8. (Them, These) textbooks are needed in class today.
9. Unfortunately, I make (this, these) types of errors whenever I type.
10. (That, Those) sort of clothes can not be worn in the office.
11. Pedro does not like (this, these) types of shoes.
12. The company wants to buy out (this, this here) business.
13. Please hand (that, that there) report to the secretary.
14. Priscilla wanted to save (this, these) kind of article.
15. The supervisor wanted (them, those) employees to work overtime.
16. (That, Those) memos must be typed before noon today.
17. (This, This here) restaurant is my favorite.
18. (This, These) sort of idea is just what the teacher wanted.
19. (That, Those) kinds of remarks will not improve our customer relations.
20. (That, That there) student received an A+ on his English final.

REPLAY DRILL 38

Select the article a or an to put in front of the following words.

Example

(<u>a</u>, an) hungry teenager

1. (a, an) yellow raincoat
2. (a, an) umbrella
3. (a, an) ten-key calculator
4. (a, an) honorable gentleman
5. (a, an) IRS agent
6. (a, an) 18 percent increase
7. (a, an) personal computer
8. (a, an) unified agreement
9. (a, an) M & M candy lover
10. (a, an) one-way street
11. (a, an) heavy package
12. (a, an) angry customer
13. (a, an) unknown author
14. (a, an) librarian
15. (a, an) USC football player
16. (a, an) early riser
17. (a, an) universal policy
18. (a, an) holiday greeting
19. (a, an) omelette
20. (a, an) one-horse town

REPLAY DRILL 39

Select the correct word for each sentence. Remember to avoid two negatives in the same sentence.

Example

I do not want (no, any) potatoes.

1. (Nobody, Everybody) won't get his or her test papers back today.
2. Mary doesn't want (no, any) chicken.
3. The store (can't, can) hardly keep those shoes in stock.
4. Stanley hasn't gone (nowhere, anywhere) in this new car.
5. I won't (never, ever) speak to Helen again.
6. Since you are on a diet, you don't need (no, any) hot fudge sundae.
7. Johnny doesn't know (nothing, anything) about Russia.
8. Mrs. French won't go (nowhere, anywhere) without her dog.
9. There was hardly (no, any) difference between the two bids on the school.
10. Linda said she wouldn't (never, ever) cheat on her diet.
11. Nobody (can, can't) leave class early today.
12. Susan scarcely (ever, never) sews anymore.
13. Don't put (none, any) gravy on my potatoes.
14. Mr. Langley doesn't need (no, any) help with the proposals.
15. I shouldn't go (anywhere, nowhere) with all this work to do.
16. Bob (can't, can) barely see in the fog.
17. Mr. Bowles can't get (any, none) of his report written with all the noise.
18. The baseball player (could, couldn't) seldom hit the curve ball.
19. Our family doesn't (never, ever) go to that restaurant to eat.
20. That child shouldn't eat (no, any) more candy.

REPLAY DRILL 40

Select the appropriate adjective for each sentence.

Example

Mrs. Brown is the (nicer, <u>nicest</u>) teacher I know.

1. We had the (goodest, best) seats in the field house.
2. Mr. Little is a (kind, kinder) man.
3. Frank is a (gooder, better) worker than his brother.
4. The Browns' new baby is a (pretty, prettier) child.
5. Alison is the (friendlier, friendliest) person in our neighborhood.
6. Which star do you think is shining the (brighter, brightest)?
7. Miss Booth is a very (efficient, efficienter) worker.
8. Kelly performed a (harder, hardest) dive than Amy did.
9. Benjamen is a (fast, faster) reader than Jonathan.
10. Bernadette is a (quick, quicker) learner.
11. Here is a (more recent, most recent) picture of my children.
12. That statue is the (less valuable, least valuable) of all the statues in the collection.
13. Rich walked (farther, farthest) than his wife.
14. This is the (baddest, worst) soup I have ever tasted.
15. Marilyn had (less, least) money than Dan.
16. Raymond is the (older, oldest) of all his brothers and sisters.
17. The rooms in this house are (wider, widest) than those in the other house.
18. The view from the top of the Empire State Building is the (more beautiful, most beautiful) I have ever seen.
19. Barbara is (younger, youngest) than her sister Ellen.
20. This peach has the (sweeter, sweetest) taste.

REPLAY BONUS DRILL 41

Decide which is needed—an adjective or an adverb—in the following sentences. Then select the correct word from the choices given.

Example

She walked (quick, <u>quickly</u>) to her car.

1. The mother sang (soft, softly) to her baby.
2. Marilyn's new dress looks (expensive, expensively).
3. The decorations on the cake are (sure, very) pretty.
4. The (swift, swiftly) current pulled the raft out to sea.
5. When the rain started, the couple walked (rapid, rapidly) to the shelter.
6. Those cookies tasted (delicious, deliciously).
7. Andrew totaled the figures (accurate, accurately).
8. The driver felt (bad, badly) about the accident.
9. The nursery school teacher was (patient, patiently) with the small children.
10. The baker decorated the cake (beautiful, beautifully).
11. The kindergarten children ran (happy, happily) into the school room.
12. Edna works (busy, busily) behind the cash register.
13. Frances' new hairstyle is (pretty, prettily).
14. This is a (real, really) diamond.
15. The students worked (real, really) hard on their science project.
16. Our doctor always writes his prescriptions (clear, clearly).
17. All criminals are entitled to a (fair, fairly) trial by law.
18. This lemon tastes (sour, sourly).
19. I am (sure, surely) you can still get tickets.
20. I have learned all the answers (well, good).

48   Student Prep Book

REPLAY DRILL 42

Each of the following sentences contains an error in the use of an adjective or adverb. Underline the error and make the necessary corrections.

Example

Paula has the whiter teeth of all the dentist's patients.   whitest

1. He writes best than George.

2. Lauren speaks good.

3. This homemade ice cream tastes deliciously.

4. Our manager runs an efficienter office.

5. The math teacher explained the rules more logically.

6. The carpenter stayed late than anyone else.

7. The child felt safely with her Dad's arm around her.

8. Greg types fastly than Yvonne.

9. If the team works together, it can get the job done quicker.

10. This milk tastes sourly.

11. The actor was very calmly before her performance.

12. Your new home is sure decorated nicely.

13. This fragrance is wider used than the others.

14. Since it was repaired, the car engine runs smoother.

15. Of all of the stockbrokers, he has the better reputation.

16. He looks very handsomely in his new suit.

17. Ruth checked over her answers careful.

18. Before going to sleep, Martin likes to read quiet.

19. The doctor ran swift to the patient's room.

20. Henry was promoted rapid in the company.

CHAPTER 8
THE TAMING OF THE APOSTROPHE

REPLAY DRILL 43

Underline the noun which is the possessor of the other noun in the following word groups. Note: apostrophes have been left out.

Example

the <u>authors</u> new book

1. the <u>childs</u> hungry friends
2. the little <u>engines</u> whistle
3. a very angry <u>customers</u> complaint
4. an honorable <u>judges</u> decision
5. a hazy <u>afternoons</u> shower
6. the two <u>factories</u> contracts
7. the gossipy <u>secretaries</u> whispers
8. two <u>months</u> interest
9. a sale on <u>childrens</u> clothes
10. <u>Virginias</u> improving economy
11. the two <u>mens</u> derby hadt
12. our <u>companys</u> insurance policy
13. the five <u>accountants</u> calculations
14. a six <u>months</u> postponement
15. a <u>years</u> worth of interest
16. the tired <u>womans</u> shopping bag
17. the happy <u>employees</u> pay raise
18. the <u>Europeans</u> accent
19. the singing <u>waiters</u> song
20. the honor <u>students</u> grade point average

READ DRILL 44

Select the correct noun in the following sentences.

Example

The (ladies', ladies) went to lunch.

1. The (secretary's, secretaries) flowers sat on her desk.

2. The (men's mens') conference is scheduled for two o'clock.

3. The (bosses', bosses) are planning to leave early today.

4. The (Booth's, Booths') party will be next Saturday.

5. Our computer (repairman's, repairmans) truck just pulled up.

6. The busy (clerks, clerks') hurried to fill the orders.

7. The new (employee's, employees') first day was very hectic.

8. Our (company's, companies') annual picnic will be in September.

9. The (freshman's, freshmans') composition was read out loud by the instructor.

10. The (professor's, professors') lecture was presented on the satellite.

11. She went to her (mother-in-law's, mother-in-laws') house for dinner.

12. The (congresswoman's, congresswomans') vote enabled the passage of the new highway bill.

13. The (child's, childs') tooth was under his pillow.

14. Several new (member's, members) were inducted into the society.

15. Do you know the (Williams', Williamses)?

16. The two (actresses', actresses) were sisters in the play.

17. The (tenants', tenants) rights had been violated by the landlord.

18. A two (month's, months') construction delay caused the college to open late.

19. Both (director's, directors) presented their ideas to the review board.

20. (Today's, Todays') weather forecast is for sunny skies and mild temperatures.

English for Careers 51

BONUS DRILL 45

Insert apostrophes where needed.

1. The children carved a jack-o'-lantern for Halloween.
2. John can't go to the movie tonight.
3. Most games at our school start at seven o'clock.
4. We'll be here today, but not tomorrow.
5. Don't you think that new baby is cute?
6. It's so cold this morning that my teeth are chattering.
7. Mary is planning on buying three IRAs before she retires.
8. Susan had nothing better to do so she counted all the a's and s's on the page.
9. Bob is studying the probabilities of 7s and 11s coming up on the roll of the dice.
10. Early rock music was played in the '50s and '60s era.
11. Jean is planning to attend the Four C's meeting this spring.
12. Robert was pleased to get six A's on his final report card.
13. The RNs on the surgical wing work very hard and are seriously understaffed.
14. Won't you be able to go to the party next week?
15. Seven CPAs have offices in that office building.
16. Be sure to cross your t's and dot your i's.
17. I wouldn't drive at night in that old car.
18. Two gymnasts received perfect 10s in the Olympics.
19. The class of '90 will have its reunion at the picnic grounds next month.
20. The instructions said that the user had to mark all the v's.

CHAPTER 9
THE PAUSE THAT REFRESHES

REPLAY DRILL 46

Underline the series in the following sentences. Then add the necessary commas. If no commas are needed, write C.

Example

I bought milk butter and eggs.   milk, butter, and eggs

1. Tonight, Chris must study English accounting and payroll.

2. The instructor said to be organized to speak clearly and to show enthusiasm.

3. The company president and the managers and the supervisor were in conference.

4. On our vacation we traveled to Washington Philadelphia and New York City.

5. Phyllis needed to find books about child abuse single-parent families and homeless shelters.

6. The students their parents and their teachers are planning the museum trip.

7. The chefs the cooks and the waiters celebrated the opening of the new restaurant.

8. All customers must wear shoes shirts and long pants in the new nightclub.

9. Please bring a main dish vegetable and dessert to the picnic.

10. The secretary's task was to type to proofread and to mail the reports.

11. Please do not fold bend or staple the enclosed payment form.

12. The board will be meeting October 5 November 9 and January 15.

13. Pineapples, kiwis and mangos are all available in local markets.

14. Harrison had to pay his rent phone bill and electric bill.

15. Mrs. Swanson buys her meats at Super Fresh her produce at Farm Fresh and her grocery items at Food Lion.

16. The young actor's parents agent and director discussed his future.

17. The family went swimming boating and snorkeling on vacation.

18. The police searched the streets the alleys and the buildings near the robbery.

19. The surgeon the lab technician and the radiologist discussed the patient's prognosis.

20. In August my friend will celebrate her birthday her anniversary and her daughter's wedding.

REPLAY DRILL 47

Insert a comma where needed in the following sentences. You will need to put a comma in a "series" or between an "adjectives only."

Example

Mason wiped the hot sticky sauce off his fingers.   hot, sticky

1. The elderly residents stayed inside because of the hot humid weather.

2. They drove the old battered dumptruck to the junkyard.

3. Tommy took a bite of the chocolate chewy candy bar.

4. For her recipe Barbie needed two eggs one stick of butter and two cups of flour.

5. Her father's bright cheery smile cheered up Melissa.

6. Linda longed for a day to enjoy the warm gentle ocean breezes.

7. The dentist told Sam he could not eat any hard crunchy foods.

8. The FBI accepts only intelligent competent applicants.

9. Elena wants ketchup mustard and relish on her hot dog.

10. Margaret's accurate efficient accounting skills led to her promotion.

11. Many soldiers were killed during the long fierce battle.

12. The friendly honest stranger returned my pocketbook.

13. When Kerry got the cast off her foot, she wanted to run to jump and to dance.

14. Her mother's note told Joanie to dust the furniture to peel the potatoes and to iron the shirts.

15. Keith's daring competent actions during the fire were praised by the mayor.

16. His ridiculous comic behavior made everyone laugh.

17. Patricia craved the hot salty taste of the freshly roasted peanuts.

18. The owner gave the first five customers a rose a $100 gift certificate and a big smile.

19. The city's new operating system accounting procedures and auditing methods will be installed this week.

20. The novice skateboarder skinned his knee bruised his arm and broke his front tooth in the accident.

REPLAY DRILL 48

Insert any necessary commas in the following sentences.

Example

I want to go to the movies yet I have to finish my composition first.   , yet

1. Please give me your test paper and you may then begin reading Chapter 5.

2. Susan baked some chocolate-chip cookies and she gave some to all the people in our group.

3. We were ready to go to class but Buddy couldn't get the car started.

4. Brenda worked quickly yet the class ended before she completed the test.

5. The secretary answered the telephone but on one was on the line.

6. The baseball player hit the ball hard and he ran quickly to first base.

7. I don't want to study but I don't want to flunk the test.

8. Alex does not want to go to the meeting nor will he be ready to leave.

9. Peggy waited by the phone for the interviewer said he would call today.

10. Are you going to buy the shoes the purse or the hat?

11. The toddlers built a sandcastle but the waves washed it away.

12. Bob gobbled down the two hamburgers and then he ate three orders of french fries.

13. Angela was on a diet yet she still managed to eat the strawberry shortcake.

14. The minister preached a good sermon but several people still fell asleep.

15. James sent in his reservation for he planned on attending the banquet.

16. The applicant was not prepared for the typing test nor could she verify her typing speed.

17. The young girl enjoyed her first plane ride and she asked the flight attendant if she could fly again.

18. William bought a ticket yet he did not attend the concert.

19. Catherine wanted to be a basketball player and she practiced her shooting every day.

20. My friend was angry for the hairstylist had cut her hair too short.

REPLAY DRILL 49

Insert any necessary commas in the following sentences.

Example

When we were in Atlanta we visited Stone Mountain.   Atlanta, we

1. Yes I'll give your papers back on Monday.

2. Mrs. Smithers can you help me with this problem?

3. In the early morning before dawn Rich went fishing.

4. If you arrive after the play begins you must wait till the usher can seat you.

5. No I am not working overtime tonight.

6. Since you will be the first to arrive would you please set up the chairs for the meeting?

7. Mr. Bryant could you get a temporary worker for me for next Friday?

8. Before leaving for work I did the laundry and washed the dishes.

9. After the thunderstorm stopped the sun came out.

10. Since going to his reunion Jerry has renewed acquaintanceships with his high school buddies.

11. Once outside the man lit up a cigarette.

12. Well I am not sure if I can go with you this weekend.

13. When I attended business school I learned to use WordPerfect.

14. Under the chair by the door Mickey found his missing glasses.

15. Oh I can't believe it's Monday already.

16. Arriving late for work Paula rushed up the steps.

17. Mr. Olivas when is our final exam?

18. When Suzie came in the door everyone shouted at her.

19. The girls shopped for hours at the mall and then they went to the movies.

20. Curtis had a lot of work to do yet he still had time to play ball with his son.

REPLAY DRILL 50

Insert the necessary commas in the following sentences. Remember, you are looking for parenthetical expressions.

Example

Mrs. Brown wants to speak however with our manager.   , however,

1. My son who likes to surf is a good swimmer. (I have one son.)

2. We would like to ask you Mr. Harvey to speak at our graduation.

3. My college roommate Toni Heiser writes faithfully each month.

4. Our reference book *Guide to Business Careers* is on hold at the library.

5. Any person young or old is invited to the festivities at the park.

6. The lottery winner who is my brother-in-law will spend his earnings wisely.

7. Can you fix the jammed copier Mr. Pope?

8. The city manager Mr. Orton will meet with the area civic leagues.

9. Our math textbook *Understanding Business Mathematics* explains how to round off decimals.

10. Give an answer yes or no about attending the seminar next week.

11. The mayor who is also a dentist was re-elected last fall.

12. The Phillies my favorite baseball team have won sixteen games in a row in Philadelphia.

13. Have you made any plans for your retirement Mr. Hunting?

14. My childhood friend Janet Sturn is visiting us next week.

15. Because of your patience with children Mrs. Norfleet I know you'll be a good day-care worker.

16. Have you read Danielle Steel's new book *Wings*?

17. I would like ladies and gentlemen to now introduce our speaker.

18. Our French teacher who is also my aunt grew up outside of Paris.

19. The encyclopedia salesman Mr. Breeden urged my parents to buy the complete set.

20. Have you met the new president of the college Dr. Morgan?

REPLAY DRILL 51

Insert the necessary commas in the following sentences.

Example

Our wedding was on August 15 1979 in Philadelphia.   August 15, 1979,

1. Mary Alice lived in Norfolk Virginia with her grandparents.

2. The children's museum in Washington D.C. has a new exhibition on safety.

3. The exchange student from Madrid Spain will live with the Kennedys.

4. Both his parents graduated on June 12 1975 from Penn State University.

5. My dentist James Kail D.D.S. has just opened his own practice.

6. The award ceremony on August 25 1991 was televised nationally.

7. My dad always says that San Francisco California is the most beautiful city in America.

8. Have you visited Disneyland in Anaheim California or Disney World in Orlando Florida?

9. James Little Ph.D. spoke to our psychology class.

10. His birthday September 6 1974 is the same date as his uncle's birthday.

11. Did your brother live in Portsmouth New Hampshire or in Portsmouth Virginia?

12. John McGuire M.D. received his graduate degree from the University of Virginia.

13. On October 14 1989 the stock market suffered a severe loss in trading.

14. Will the yearly conference be in Tampa Florida or Charleston South Carolina?

15. Classes will begin on Thursday September 5 1991.

16. On November 15 1989 John's father retired after thirty years with the company.

17. Both John P. Smith Ph.D. and William R. Smith M.D. paid for a world cruise for their parents.

18. The train left from Richmond Viriginia and traveled to Montreal Canada.

19. The conference will begin on Monday October 5 and end on Wednesday October 12.

20. Muriel Freeman M.D. will be the guest lecturer at the Pavilion in Longport Rhode Island.

REPLAY DRILL 52

Decide if the commas used in the following sentences are correct and if additional commas may be needed. If the sentences are correct, write (C). If a comma is used incorrectly, underline the mistake; if a comma is needed, insert it.

Example

Her mother said "No, you can't stay home from school today."   said,

1. "Can you come to work early on Friday,?" asked Mrs. Lincoln.

2. "You may go," his father said, "but be home by midnight."

3. My grandmother always told me, "Don't wish your life away; it will go by fast enough on its own."

4. "Please" the professor said, "use specific examples to prove your answers."

5. Frank shouted, "Watch out!," and ran to grab the child from the path of the oncoming car.

6. His friends yelled "Surprise" when Al came into the restaurant.

7. "Are you exempt from taking the final exam in English?" asked Mrs. Franklin.

8. Greg kept answering every question with "I don't know."

9. The supervisor instructed "Everyone must complete the questionnaire in fifteen minutes."

10. "All the students clapped after my speech," Georgeanna exclaimed.

11. Instead of saying he would take the job, the applicant just said, "maybe."

12. "Thanks for tutoring me in English, Mrs. Edgars," said Timothy.

13. Lana's friends yelled, "Goodbye" as her bus pulled out of the station.

14. "Who will drive the carpool van next week,?" asked Mr. Lewis.

15. "Since the bank is closing," the manager explained, "you must take your savings to another bank."

16. "Can you believe this gorgeous view!" Melissa yelled.

17. Marvin asked "When will the word processing seminar begin on Saturday?"

18. When Lester finished his speech, the audience yelled "Hurray!"

19. The student replied, "The word group is not a complete thought; therefore, it is a fragment."

20. When his father gave him the keys to the new car, John could only say, "Wow!"

REPLAY DRILL 53-A

Insert the necessary commas in the following sentences. If a comma is not needed, write C.

Example

A long long time passed before she answered his proposal.   long, long

1. Chris wants to skateboard not to study.
2. Halloween is October 31 not October 30.
3. Anne always works very very hard on all of her assignments.
4. The couple does the weekly shopping on Saturday never on Sunday.
5. Everyone passed the exam but Craig.
6. It was a sunny sunny day in California.
7. Kenny eats eggs for breakfast never cereal.
8. Mr. Lawrence often travels to London seldom to Paris.
9. If you are going to walk walk quickly.
10. Maurice is always early for work never late.
11. The delegate will arrive tomorrow morning not afternoon.
12. When you speak speak loudly.
13. Dean gave the answer to Connie not Wendy.
14. She worked overtime for two hours not three.
15. I always go shopping with Laura never Samantha.
16. Albert wanted buttered popcorn not plain.
17. All the neighbors made a contribution but not the Lankfords.
18. My mother always bakes cakes seldom pies.
19. The librarian handed the books to Walt not Steve.
20. Robin always listens to WABC never to WCDF.

REPLAY DRILL 53-B

Using the rules in Units 49-56, insert commas in the following sentences. Five sentences are correct.

Example

enrollment of 12000   12,000

1. Marjory grew up at 516 Belmont Avenue Chicago Illinois.

2. The answers are on page 947.

3. Leigh studied for her exams till midnight but she still had trouble falling asleep.

4. My son graduated from high school on June 13 1991.

5. Yes I'll work overtime next Wednesday.

6. The new dean Mrs. Tieg will meet with all the faculty.

7. When she left the office Ellen ran to catch to bus.

8. Everyone went to the basketball game but Leon.

9. The children played in the sandbox splashed in the kiddie pool and ran around the backyard.

10. Ms. Powers is a fast accurate typist.

11. Sally is well educated yet she has no common sense.

12. The city engineer of course will speak about the downtown road improvement project.

13. The company vice president George Hampton shook everyone's hand as he entered the room.

14. How many hours will it take to drive from Boston Massachusetts to Charlotte North Carolina?

15. If you work for this company you will be required to travel several times a week.

16. The bank manager announced, "Our branch offices will be open Saturday mornings starting in September."

17. Mr. Williams are you leaving for Denver this afternoon or this evening?

18. The disc jockey played several records and he reported on the day's news highlights.

19. We expected delivery by September 1 not October 1.

20. The lost merchandise was from Invoice No. 14576-B.

CHAPTER 10
PUNCTUATION POTPOURRI

REPLAY DRILL 54

Insert the correct punctuation mark at the end of the following. Use either a period, question mark, or exclamation mark.

Example

Do you have practice tomorrow (?)

1. Please present your report to the committee
2. Excellent work
3. Would you please come by my office at 5 o'clock
4. Are you able to complete this work by noon
5. Great idea
6. The supervisor asked if you would be there
7. I wonder if the employees will get a raise
8. Do you know how to videotape my speech
9. Terrific
10. Frank asked when you would be ready to leave
11. Would you help me with this math problem
12. Thanks, John, for a job well done
13. What a fantastic report
14. Watch out
15. John wondered what time the seminar would end
16. May I have your reply by tomorrow morning
17. Martha asked if you enjoyed your new job
18. I am looking forward to working with you
19. You won
20. Would December 1 or December 2 be the better date to meet

REPLAY DRILL 55

Insert the semicolons and commas where needed in the following sentences.

Example

Avis is an excellent student she studies hard.   student;

1. Doctor Hobley, who was our mayor, will speak at the meeting he is an excellent speaker.
2. Sabrina ran toward the bus then she suddenly dropped all her packages.
3. Harold was hurt in an accident therefore he missed three weeks of work.
4. The young couple saved every penny they could nevertheless it took them ten years to save for a home.
5. The company promised its employees a raise that is each person would receive a five percent increase.
6. Mom works hard at her job then she comes home to prepare dinner.
7. The motion was passed by the City Council the vote was 6 to 3.
8. Bessie Cambria, my former neighbor, is coming to town and she will stay with our family.
9. Phil worked overtime for three months hence he was glad to get home early.
10. Mr. Leslie has worked for our company for thirty years therefore he is eligible for retirement.
11. Three players got base hits still the team could not score any runs.
12. Angela works two different jobs also she volunters for the literacy council.
13. The retired couple cashed in their savings bonds thus they could afford the world cruise.
14. Mr. Barrows came to work early yet he still did not complete all the work.
15. We traveled to Cambridge, Massachusetts Portsmouth New Hampshire and Augusta Maine.
16. Joanna wanted a raise however she was afraid to ask her supervisor.
17. Mr. Johnson completed a speech course nevertheless he was still nervous when he stood in front of the audience.
18. It is Mr. Bell's birthday his friends are planning a surprise party.
19. The company received a multimillion dollar contract therefore they will be hiring new employees.
20. Two of the panelists started arguing thus the moderator had to intervene to continue the discussion.

REPLAY DRILL 56

Insert the colons where they are needed in the following sentences. Write C for the two sentences that do not require a colon.

Example
We need to buy the following supplies: pens, folders, and envelopes.

1. Each set of silverware includes these utensils twelve salad forks, twelve dinner forks, twelve spoons, and twelve knives.
2. Sunrise will be at 5 45 a.m. tomorrow morning.
3. Karen's goals were Graduation Career Marriage
4. Peter had one thought in mind food.
5. When you use mixed punctuation in a sentence, the salutation should be Gentlemen or Ladies and Gentlemen.
6. We can schedule the banquet on February 8, February 15, or March 1.
7. The word processing seminar will begin at 8 30 a.m. and break for lunch at 11 45 a.m.
8. After working a 12-hour shift, Maggie was looking forward to one thing sleep.
9. Please send the following by United Parcel 100 reams of copy paper and four quarts of toner.
10. The following people were elected to a City Council Matthew Lawrence, Madeline Booth, and Stevie Highes.
11. Employers rank three job qualifications the highest appearance, dependability, and skills.
12. Jonathan received double-time for working three holidays Thanksgiving, Christmas, and New Year's Day.
13. The annual company picnic will begin at 11 30 a.m., Friday morning.
14. Bring the following supplies with you to class some typing paper, a manila folder, and a good dictionary.
15. Benjamin Franklin wrote, "A penny saved is a penny earned."
16. Chris has to eliminate eating the following foods while on his diet candy, ice cream, and snack foods.
17. The advertising circular featured many specials Ground Beef Whole Chickens Sirloin Steak
18. Three interviewees were called back for second interviews Betty Mandez, Avis Bartlett, and Dan Baker.
19. Be sure to attend our Grand Opening April 7, April 8, and April 9.
20. Registration will begin at 8 00, and the seminar will begin at 8 30.

REPLAY DRILL 57

Put the quotation marks where they are needed in the following sentences.

Example

When she completed her exams, Mallory exclaimed, "Hurray!"

1. Many students confuse accept with except.
2. Say I can instead of I can't.
3. Thank you, Mr. Lockner, Ryan said sincerely.
4. Look for the silver lining in every cloud.
5. Charlie yelled, We're lost!
6. Please read the chapter entitled Uses for Quotation Marks in your text.
7. What time will your plane arrive? Dale asked.
8. Martin was chosen Employee of the Year in 1990.
9. The crowd cheered, We won!
10. Did you mean eligible or illegible?
11. The article Money Management in this morning's paper gave me some good ideas.
12. His friends told the actor to break a leg.
13. Don't use ain't in formal business communications.
14. Mitch asked, Are you working overtime tonight?
15. The refrigerator magnet read, Don't Feed Me!
16. The play Les Miserables is touring throughout the United States.
17. April wondered, Should I order dessert?
18. Never use irregardless in your writing; it's a nonstandard word form.
19. The umpire yelled, Play ball!
20. The surfers hoped they could catch a wave today.

REPLAY DRILL 58

Put the necessary hyphens where they belong in the following word groups. Write C for the one in which hyphens are not needed, and join the one that should be written solid.

Example

seventy seven students   seventy-seven students

1. an up to date weather report
2. first rate accommodations
3. my editor in chief's report
4. his lack of self respect
5. the out of stock sale item
6. a four year college
7. a ten story office building
8. a hard to find location
9. a part time position
10. a high priced antique
11. ninety nine percent of the vote
12. a mid July white sale
13. the quality of self control
14. the well dressed executive
15. six foot sections
16. my brother in law's new car
17. a kind hearted individual
18. high risk investment
19. third class postage rate
20. Larry's self respect

REPLAY DRILL 59

Add the apostrophe where it is needed in the following word groups.

Example

Sid scorecard   Sid's scorecard

1. two weeks pay
2. Mr. Hernandez car
3. the childrens bike
4. the childs skateboard
5. the bosss memo
6. the secretaries desks
7. someones briefcase
8. Janices typewriter
9. a womans rights
10. the ladies pocketbooks
11. Benjamin Franklins experiments
12. Jamess report card
13. both authors opinions
14. my mother-in-laws cooking
15. three months interest
16. the employees coffee break
17. the Prime Ministers address
18. the two companies merger
19. the Joneses party
20. the teachers lounge

BONUS DRILL 60

Part One   Put the parentheses where they are needed in the following sentences.

Example

John (my sister's first husband) is coming for dinner.

1. I worked hard believe me to complete this assignment.

2. We will go not now to the research library.

3. The dress cost $49 not $59.

4. The bank's Saturday hours 9 to noon will soon be changed.

5. The decimal equivalents see Figure 4, page 80 will help you with the percentages.

6. These VCRs last year's models are reduced.

7. Reverend Chamberlain our first minister is coming to Suzanne's wedding.

8. It will be Wendy not her sister who will be maid of honor.

9. The state postal abbreviations see chart, page 23 should be used on all envelopes.

10. The new Food Carnival the one near the mall has the best selection of meats.

Part Two   Put the dashes where they belong in the following sentences.

Example

The company party is Saturday--I can't wait!

11. Please make a donation we need your help now.

12. Happiness it's yours for the asking.

13. He won money a great deal of money by playing the lottery each week.

14. Our new refrigerator rated number one by Consumer Reports has an icemaker and water dispenser.

15. Our supervisor a real sweetheart gave us the afternoon off.

16. The new board members Dr. Duzeck and Ms. Swenson will meet with the press this afternoon.

17. Crack thousands of babies have been born addicted.

18. Style, grace, and beauty the beauty pageant winner had them all!

19. Sharmita she was the winner praised her parents for their love and devotion.

20. The new personal computer the color printer is included is the best value of the year.

CHAPTER 11
A BUSINESS DICTIONARY

REPLAY DRILL 61

Choose the correct response from the terms listed below to fill in the blanks.

1. The outside accountants worked for several weeks to determine the correctness of the _____.

2. Mary Jones designated her daughter the _____ of her life insurance policy.

3. The stock market prices have been declining in this _____.

4. Since Mr. Jones did not pay his debts, the creditors secured an _____.

5. The Smith family wanted the realtor to give an exact _____ of their property.

6. If the goods are not listed on the _____, then the company probably did not send it.

7. The computer's memory stores a group of bits equal to this unit of information. _____

8. The merger of two or more businesses into one is also called an _____.

9. This is the summary of the business to be taken up at a meeting. _____

10. The _____ gave an accurate estimate of the damage to Bill's car.

    A. byte   **E.** agenda   **I.** beneficiary
    B. bear market   **F.** audit   **J.** amalgamation
    C. adjuster   **G.** attachment   **K.** bull market
    D. appraisal   **H.** bill of lading

REPLAY DRILL 62

Choose the correct response from the terms listed below to fill in the blanks.

1. The company required a _____ check before they release the order to the new customer.

2. Mr. Smith's credit was so bad that he had to put up _____ in order to secure the loan.

3. The neighborhood houses had suffered from so much _____ that their values were in great decline.

4. This modern technique has saved millions of dollars in typesetting and layout costs. _____

5. Stock market enthusiasts listen for the closing prices of 65 stocks on the New York Stock Exchange called the _____.

6. This method of sending and receiving messages through telephone lines and computers is _____.

7. The study of equipment, furniture, and physical environment, called _____, makes the workplace more comfortable, safer, and more conducive to employee efficiency.

8. Lucky employees have companies that put aside money for them in this plan. _____

9. The bank examiners discovered the misappropriation of funds in the _____ scheme.

10. All of the money paid out by the company is called _____.

A. Dow Jones Average
B. ergonomics
C. certified
D. depreciation
E. embezzlement
F. electronic mail
G. collateral
H. profit sharing
I. desktop publishing
J. disbursements

REPLAY DRILL 63

Choose the correct response from the terms listed below to fill in the blanks.

1. Electronic transmission of copies of documents, photographs, drawings, signatures, etc., over telephone lines is called a _____.

2. The rise and fall, as of prices, is _____.

3. The value of the public relations of a business is considered the _____.

4. The written travel plan showing arrival and departure times and hotel reservations is a business person's _____.

5. Closing a business and selling its assets in order to turn the assets into cash is _____.

6. Being unable to pay one's debt is being _____.

7. The data put into information processing systems is _____.

8. The vast national and international computer network linking individuals, universities, businesses, and government agencies for exchanging information is _____.

9. The obligations or debts of a business or a person are _____.

10. _____ is the process of engaging in a lawsuit or legal action.

    A. liquidation   **F.** fax
    B. insolvent   **G.** good will
    C. fluctuation   **H.** Internet
    D. litigation   **I.** input
    E. itinerary   **J.** liabilities

REPLAY DRILL 64

Choose the correct response from the terms listed below to fill in the blanks.

1. McDonald's has opened restaurants in several countries this year; therefore, it is a _____ corporation.

2. John was astonished when he saw his first paycheck because there were so many deductions. His _____ pay was much lower than he had anticipated.

3. The instructor used laser disks and music from compact disks to enhance the lesson ever since she had taken the _____ course.

4. Collaborative learning can be accomplished by a group of students if their computers are joined together by a _____.

5. Mrs. Jones would like to buy that land, so she has asked the company for an _____ to purchase it.

6. It is necessary to have a _____ in order to transmit messages on the e-mail.

7. The owner of the jewelry store had a huge _____ on the price of the new gold necklaces.

8. The salesman had a _____ allowance for his daily expenses.

9. The elderly man was so ill that he had to give _____ to his son to conduct business affairs.

10. The _____ affixed her seal to the legal documents.

A. power-of-attorney
B. markup
C. network
D. multinational
E. modem
F. gross
G. net
H. multimedia
I. notary public
J. overhead
K. option
L. per diem

REPLAY DRILL 65

Choose the correct response from the terms listed below to fill in the blanks.

1. The owner of the stock could not be present for the annual meeting, so he asked that his shares be voted by _____.

2. Susan placed 1000 sheets of paper in the copy machine which was equal to two _____.

3. Harold wants to install new accounting and payroll _____ on his computer.

4. The government will issue new _____ on cars imported from Japan and Germany this year.

5. Mary worked for a long time to find the error in her checkbook so that the _____ would be correct.

6. The company has been making a good profit this year and paying their bills on time; therefore, they are _____.

7. The supervisor filled out seven _____ for the purchase of supplies he needed in the office.

8. If the speaker is quoted word for word, it is _____.

9. Robert put the wrong amount on the receipt, so he had to _____ it and issue a new one.

10. Sylvia paid the lawyer $1,000 as a _____ to be sure he would defend her in the future.

    A. hardware   G. proxy
    B. solvent   H. reconciliation
    C. reams   I. requisitions
    D. verbatim   J. retainer
    E. tariffs   K. void
    F. via   L. software

BONUS DRILL 66

One spelling is correct. Write the letter of the correct spelling.

_____ 1. (a) affidavid   (b) afidavit   (c) affidavit

_____ 2. (a) byte   (b) bite   (c) bide

_____ 3. (a) colateral   (b) colatteral   (c) collateral

_____ 4. (a) equity   (b) equidy   (c) equitty

_____ 5. (a) argonomics   (b) ergonomics   (c) ergomonics

_____ 6. (a) fluxuation   (b) flucation   (c) flucuation

_____ 7. (a) itinerary   (b) itemerary   (c) itinary

_____ 8. (a) moden   (b) modem   (c) modum

_____ 9. (a) multimedia   (b) ultimeduim   (c) multinedia

_____ 10. (a) remitance   (b) remittence   (c) remittance

Choose the correct pronunciation.

_____ 11. amalgamation   (a) a mal guh ma shun   (b) uh mal guh ma shun

_____ 12. lien   (a) leen   (b) line

_____ 13. diem   (a) dee um   (b) die um

_____ 14. bytes   (a) bits   (b) bites

_____ 15. libel   (a) li uh bl   (b) li bl

_____ 16. quorum   (a) kor um   (b) kwor um

_____ 17. verbatim   (a) ver bayt um   (b) ver bat um

_____ 18. reprographics   (a) re pro graf ics   (b) rep ro graf ics

_____ 19. rider   (a) rid der   (b) rid er

_____ 20. fiscal   (a) fisk el   (b) fis kil

CHAPTER 12
WEATHER OR KNOT

REPLAY DRILL 67

Underscore the correct word to complete the following sentences.

Example

Please (ad, <u>add</u>) these numbers correctly.

1. Jose planned to take another (coarse, course) in accounting.

2. Ted needed a (fiscal, physical) exam to be eligible to play football.

3. The child's (bizarre, bazaar) behavior upset his parents.

4. We all planned to attend the meeting (accept, except) Karen.

5. The American Cancer Society volunteer tried to (illicit, elicit) donations from our neighborhood.

6. The doctor tried to (counsel, council) the woman about her illness.

7. The Clean (Heir, Air) Commission fights against pollution.

8. Can you (here, hear) what the professor is saying?

9. The explorers made their (dissent, descent) into the cave.

10. Rob and Laura Petrie got black (die, dye) all over their hands.

11. Can you (cite, site, sight) a verse from that poem?

12. We need $3,000 in (capital, capitol) for a down payment.

13. The architect had to (alter, altar) the plans for the house.

14. What was the (affect, effect) of the storm on the shoreline?

15. Since there was an (access, excess) of material, she made matching curtains.

16. The carpenter needs a (coarse, course) grain of sandpaper.

17. The state government ran out of money before the beginning of the new (fiscal, physical) year.

18. We (accept, except) with pleasure your generous donation.

19. A great deal of (illicit, elicit) drinking occurred during Prohibition.

20. The student (counsel, council) had a car wash to raise money for a graduation party.

REPLAY DRILL 68

Underscore the correct word to complete the following sentences.

Example

(Their, There, <u>They're</u>) coming to dinner next Wednesday.

1. The criminal will (waive, wave) his rights to a trial.
2. The professor takes the class (role, roll) before starting the lecture.
3. Mr. Carlton's talk was the (principal, principle) reason we came to the convention.
4. World (peace, piece) should be every country's concern.
5. Denise's father is a (naval, navel) architect.
6. Mr. George has (led, lead) the organization for twenty-five years.
7. The dog wagged (it's, its) tail when he saw me.
8. The mechanic fixed the (minor, miner) problem with the engine of the car.
9. My grandmother has vivid memories of her (passed, past).
10. Gina had to (pear, pair, pare) the apples before making the pie.
11. The demolition crew had to (raise, raze) the old high school building to construct the shopping center.
12. The bookcases in the classroom are (stationary, stationery).
13. The magazine salesman tried to (peddle, pedal) his ware.
14. The newlyweds (residents, residence) will be in Harrisburg, Pennsylvania.
15. Try to conserve paper; do not (waist, waste) it.
16. (Your, You're) going on vacation next week, aren't you?
17. The Amish people live in our modern society by old-fashioned (principals, principles).
18. The new company needed to buy letterhead (stationery, stationary) for its new business.
19. George found out he had (passed, past) all his final exams.
20. The (residents, residence) of the retirement home were forced out of bed by the fire alarm.

REPLAY DRILL 69

Underscore the correct word to complete the following sentences.

Example

The patient was (conscience, <u>conscious</u>) shortly after surgery.

1. We had to (adapt, adopt) the blueprints to include another window.
2. Mark is (adopt, adept) at woodworking.
3. The picnic will be held (irregardless, regardless) of the weather.
4. The motorist gave (human, humane) treatment to the injured animal.
5. The sheriff's deputies tried to (envelop, envelope) the fugitive in the woods.
6. The weather forecaster announced the (eminent, imminent) arrival of the hurricane.
7. Can you (advise, advice) me as to which route is best?
8. Come sit (beside, besides) me on the bench.
9. Which dress will you (chose, choose) to wear to the party?
10. You must list your references in a (bibliography, biographical) at the end of your report.
11. The travelers got lost in the barren (desert, dessert).
12. The young couple met with a financial counselor to (device, devise) a plan to pay their bills.
13. The board decided to (defer, differ) the motion to the next meeting.
14. Corkey was (eligible, illegible) for varsity football.
15. Her (conscience, conscious) told her not to cheat on the test.
16. We will (chose, choose) a puppy from the SPCA.
17. Grant (chose, choose) to major in architecture.
18. Joe Paterno is an (eminent, imminent) college football coach.
19. The two brothers would always (defer, differ) on how to get the job done.
20. The teenager never listened to her mother's (advise, advice).

REPLAY DRILL 70

Underscore the correct word to complete the following sentences.

Example

Kirk's (moral, <u>morale</u>) was always positive and upbeat.

1. My brother could always run faster (then, than) I.
2. The (realty, reality) of his statement was verified by the witness.
3. The teacher tried to explain what had happened from the students' (perspective, prospective).
4. Did you (lose, loose) your new jacket?
5. Don't use company letterheads for your (personal, personnel) correspondence.
6. The company rents a (suit, suite) of offices in the new Dominion Towers Building.
7. Eileen was (quite, quiet) sure she would accept the job.
8. The company decided to (proceed, precede) with the new advertising campaign.
9. The paperboy decided to (persecute, prosecute) the customers who refused to pay their bills.
10. The (whether, weather) forecast for Labor Day was sunny and mild.
11. The proofreader completed a (through, thorough) job by correcting all the errors.
12. We (were, we're) planning travel to Montreal by train.
13. The (perquisite, prerequisite) for the legal terminology course is the business law course.
14. The young man spoke (respectfully, respectively) to his date's father.
15. The man credited his parents for giving him a good (moral, morale) foundation.
16. To sell homes you need a (realty, reality) license.
17. The new parents reminded the guests to be (quite, quiet) since the baby was sleeping.
18. Ramona received the application from the (personal, personnel) department.
19. The flower girl will (proceed, precede) the bride down the aisle.
20. Do not (persecute, prosecute) someone just because he or she is different.

REPLAY DRILL 71

Underscore the preposition or other errors in the following sentences.

Example

Where is it <u>at</u>?   Correct--Where is it?

1. Did you get your bracelet off of Marie?
2. Eric never should of cheated on the test.
3. The pitcher fell off of the counter.
4. The refund was split among Kelly and Stevie.
5. Betty's mother was waiting on her to come home from work.
6. Marvin sat between Carol and I on the bus.
7. Patrick must of missed the last bus.
8. The Powers family lives near to Wrigley Field.
9. Where are you going to on your vacation?
10. Did you get a telegram from she?
11. Everyone but I are going to enter the dance contest.
12. We could of scored more points if we would have taken more time.
13. Mrs. Murphy divided the ice cream between the three children.
14. Please remove those messy papers off of the kitchen table.
15. I might of gone if I had known you were going.
16. All the offensive players except I scored at least two points.
17. Please get a receipt off the waitress.
18. Now I know I should of studied harder in high school.
19. Did you receive that note off of Jenny?
20. Stephanie may of left her calculator in the accounting room.

BONUS DRILL 72

Choose the correct pronunciation. A capital letter designates the long sound of the vowel.

_____ 1. asked   (a) ast   (b) axt

_____ 2. athletics   (a) ath let iks   (b) ath e let iks

_____ 3. Des Moines   (a) de moyns   (b) de moyn

_____ 4. genuine   (a) gen u wine   (b) gen u in

_____ 5. hostile   (a) hos til   (b) hos tile

_____ 6. Illinois   (a) ill i noys   (b) ill i noy

_____ 7. Italian   (a) i tal yin   (b) I tal yin

_____ 8. naive   (a) nav   (b) ni eev

_____ 9. subtle   (a) sut l   (b) sub tl

_____ 10. versatile   (a) ver se tile   (b) ver si til

CHAPTER 13
SENTENCE POWER

REPLAY DRILL 73

Underline the dangler in the following sentences. If the sentence does not have a dangler write (C).

Example

<u>While walking through the park</u>, the wind blew my hat into the bushes.

1. Having taken too many sick days, the supervisor was forced to fire Ralph.

2. Because Ralph took too many sick days, the supervisor was forced to fire Ralph.

3. Biting quickly on the bait, the young fisherman caught his first fish.

4. Since the fish bit on the bait, the young fisherman caught his first fish.

5. The teacher read from his old textbook, which was torn around the edges.

6. Torn around the edges, the minister read from his old textbook.

7. Sitting on the windowsill, Mrs. Williams watered the geraniums.

8. Mrs. Williams watered the geraniums, which were sitting on the windowsill.

9. His mother gave John, who received good grades, tickets to a rock concert.

10. Having received good grades, his mother gave John tickets to a rock concert.

11. Being on the discount table, Ms. Jefferies saved $10 on the new gloves.

12. Ms. Jefferies saved $10 on her new gloves since they were on the discount table.

13. Because Mrs. Cunningham felt as though she was in labor, her husband took her to the hospital.

14. Feeling as though she was in labor, her husband took Mrs. Cunningham to the hospital.

15. Jogging quickly around the block, her new shoes hurt her feet.

16. While Janice was jogging around the block, her new shoes hurt her feet.

17. Before going home, this account must be audited.

18. Before you go home, this account must be audited.

19. After browsing through the store, the clerk rang up my purchases.

20. When I finished browsing through the store, the clerk rang up my purchases.

REPLAY DRILL 74

Part One   Combine these short choppy sentences into one smooth sentence.

Example

Jim likes ice cream.   Chocolate is his favorite.
Jim likes chocolate ice cream.

1. Allen went to business school. She majored in the executive secretary program.

2. Chris plays football. He is on the junior varsity team.

3. The store at the mall had a sale. It was a good sale.

4. The hamburger was juicy. It was covered with onions.

5. The clock was ticking loudly. It gave Marissa a headache.

6. He completed his homework. He had a snack.

7. Brenda read the comics. Brenda laughed.

8. Kenneth weighs 183 pounds. He decided to go on a diet.

9. Linda and Freddie went to the movies. They split a large popcorn.

10. Classes will begin on September 3. That day is also Crystal's birthday.

Part Two   Underline the vague pronoun and replace it with more specific wording.

Example

<u>They</u> require customers to were shoes and shirts.
the management

11. Mrs. Saners trained Elley on the new computer program, and she did a good job.

12. They say our taxes are due by April 15.

13. Tiffany told her mother that they were all allowed to go.

14. Helen saw Patricia talking to her daughter.

15. Mark met Frank while he was in college.

16. You must bring a textbook, notebook paper, and a folder to class.

17. Leslie's mother is a beautiful woman, and I'm sure she'll be a beauty queen too.

18. Tim was a track star in high school; it was a sport he loved.

19. You are not allowed to smoke in the theater.

20. Lance's father is a carpenter, and he will be able to build the cabinet you want.

REPLAY DRILL 75

Part One   Underline the misplaced words in the following sentences.

Example

Thelma played a hymn in church <u>by Mozart</u>.

1. Throw over the fence some hay.

2. The mother sang a lullaby with the beautiful voice.

3. The mirror was returned by the customer with the crack in the middle.

4. The ice cream was gobbled down by the children with the chocolate swirls.

5. My bike is in the garage with two flat tires.

6. The parking lot was repaved by the contractor with the speed bumps.

7. The dog buried its bone with the furry tail.

8. The student came to the school with one textbook.

9. The rose bush was pruned by the gardner with the thorns.

10. Sally searched for her pocketbook in the English classroom, which was misplaced this morning.

Part Two   If the following sentences need parallel parts, write (NP). If the sentence is correct, write (C).

Example

Susan has red hair, fair skin, and is heavily built. (C)

11. Amanda is an attorney, spends times cooking, and she loves to ski.

12. My uncle is a chef and drives an ambulance.

13. Bob would rather travel by train or ride by bus.

14. The carnival was noisy and loudly.

15. Laurie is an honor society member, a cheerleader, and sings in the school choral group.

16. The third baseman ran to first, slid into second, and scored the winning run.

17. Polly jogged down the street, across the boulevard, and over the bridge to her mother's house.

18. The play was entertaining, made us laugh, and mysterious.

19. The research specialist's talk was motivating and challenged.

20. You must write clearly and with conciseness.

REPLAY DRILL 76

Decide if the following sentences are examples of direct style (D) or indirect style (I).

Example

Jonah typed the letter.   (D)

1. The supervisor announced the new work schedule.
2. The compositions were corrected by the teacher.
3. The farmer collected antique tractors.
4. The man's name was mispronounced by all the speakers.
5. John threw the softball to his daughter.
6. The staff flew to Denver for the convention.
7. Her luggage was lost by the airlines.
8. Richard wallpapered the bathroom.
9. The airlines lost Bernadette's suitcase.
10. The telephone was answered by the department manager.
11. Mother baked your favorite dessert.
12. Too many "you knows" were used throughout the speech.
13. You should mail those contracts to the new address.
14. Last year the electric company increased rates to its residential customers.
15. The radiologist read the patient's X-ray.
16. Several mistakes were found by the editors.
17. The seminar was conducted by the personnel department.
18. The reporter presented the top news story.
19. Pan Am Airlines was bought out by Delta Airways.
20. Mr. Bell coaches his son's Little League team.

BONUS DRILL 77

Find and underline the dangling verbals in the following paragraph. Rewrite the paragraph correctly in the space provided.

While shopping at the new outlet center, the people could be seen spending lots of money. After looking for just the right dress for a long time, the clerk finally waited on me. Shopping bags filled with bargains, the girls walked outside to face the heat. Overcome by fatigue that afternoon, the stores no longer looked attractive. Having used up all their time and energy, the manager turned off the lights.

CHAPTER 14
SINCERELY YOURS

REPLAY DRILLS 78-80

Place a (T) before true statements and an (F) before false ones.

True – False

_____ 1. Large envelopes are called 9's or 10's.

_____ 2. Letters typed on a computer should be proofread on the copy.

_____ 3. The date is placed two or three lines below the printed letterhead.

_____ 4. International and Military style has the month written before the day when writing the date.

_____ 5. Official state abbreviations are never used in the inside address.

_____ 6. Double spacing between paragraphs eliminates the need to indent the first line of each new paragraph.

_____ 7. Modern business writers try to learn the name of the person they are writing to instead of writing to the attention of a department.

_____ 8. The Enclosure notice is placed two spaces above the initials of the preparer.

_____ 9. Since the age of word processing, it is unnecessary to add postscripts.

_____ 10. A bc notation always appears on the original copy of the letter.

_____ 11. In modified block style, the date and closing begin at about the horizontal center of the line.

_____ 12. A long letter of about 200 or more words requires a 70 space line for the Picture Frame Effect.

_____ 13. Zip Codes are placed on a separate line on the envelope.

_____ 14. The opening and closing paragraphs are often the longest ones in the letter.

_____ 15. Using long, sophisticated words impresses the receiver of the letter.

_____ 16. Most business letters are typed on 8 ½ by 11 paper.

_____ 17. Subject lines are usually placed two spaces below the salutation.

_____ 18. The complimentary close is a double space after the last line of the body.

_____ 19. The official job title or department name appears directly above the writer's typed name.

_____ 20. When the first line of the inside address is Mr. John Brown, an appropriate salutation would be "Dear Sir."

BONUS DRILL 81

Find the redundant and out-of-date expressions in the following letter and rewrite it in modern style.

> 725 Winding Lane
> Challenge, IO
> March 25, 1996

Mr. John Smith
246 Elm Drive
Akron, OH 44624

Dear Mr. Smith:

I am writing to inform you that we are in receipt of your recent letter dated February 26 of 1996. It is always a pleasure to hear from such a valued customer. In the aforementioned letter you stated that you were unhappy with our shipment # HN2468297 containing seven widgets. We submit our heartfelt apology for this unfortunate error. We will make every effort to rectify it.

Our shipping department will make every effort to send you the correct widgets in due course of time. I personally believe that this can be taken care of in a speedy fashion to everyone's satisfaction.

Hoping to hear from you soon, I remain,

> Faithfully yours,
>
> Robert Orderly

ANSWERS TO DRILLS

REPLAY DRILL 1-A

1. Shenita, Mark, textbook
2. students, miles, school, day
3. assignments, weeks
4. syllabi, information, subject
5. Tina, Rose, application, loan
6. Will, stomach, class
7. errors, timings
8. instructor, schedule, week
9. Larry, textbooks, notebooks, papers, backpack
10. classroom, computers, printers

REPLAY DRILL 1-B

1. She, anyone
2. your, his
3. I, their
4. who, him
5. Something, her
6. I, this
7. Everyone, their
8. He, nothing
9. You
10. Those, you, who, your
11. Whomever, you
12. her
13. her
14. Somebody, his, her
15. everyone, no one
16. she
17. I, mine, it, hers
18. We, ourselves, our
19. his, me
20. Everything

REPLAY DRILL 2

1. welcomed
2. will be attending
3. was
4. has handed
5. required
6. will be
7. were jumping
8. brightened
9. echoed
10. were looking

REPLAY DRILL 3-A

1. irritating, busy
2. tired, thirsty, cold
3. noisy, water, law
4. slippery, wooden
5. efficient, ten-page
6. magnificent, inner, office
7. elegant, new, firm
8. old, faded, torn
9. heavier, computer
10. grouchy, fresh, brewed
11. Several
12. enough
13. Twenty-five
14. no
15. few
16. These, the
17. A, this
18. The, that
19. An, those
20. This, an

REPLAY DRILL 3-B

1. finally
2. diligently
3. immediately
4. very
5. well
6. really
7. extremely
8. almost
9. appropriately
10. accurately
11. cheaply
12. never
13. hard
14. most
15. too
16. exceptionally
17. rapidly
18. so
19. not
20. now

REPLAY DRILL 4

1. but
2. when
3. until
4. so that
5. or
6. but
7. while
8. since
9. if
10. whenever
11. on the desk
12. in the folder
13. through the clouds
14. along the path
15. above the business
16. into the file cabinet
17. across the street
18. except Luther, on the business trip
19. during the lecture
20. beneath the other papers

REPLAY DRILL 5-A

1. noun
2. adjective
3. verb
4. adjective
5. verb
6. noun
7. noun
8. verb
9. adjective
10. adjective
11. verb
12. noun
13. verb
14. adjective
15. noun
16. noun
17. adjective
18. verb
19. adjective
20. verb

REPLAY DRILL 5-B

1. receptionist
2. Chris
3. children
4. composition
5. answer
6. lightning
7. picture
8. beach
9. Mr. Gomez
10. Summertime
11. clapped
12. announced
13. handcuffed
14. melted
15. raced
16. typed
17. cheered
18. tossed
19. stunned
20. flooded

BONUS DRILL 6

1. Conjunctive adverb
2. <u>even though we had driven the vehicle only 32 miles</u>
3. the need for this service apparently existed when we drove the new van out of the showroom
4. a, the, the, a
5. assume, has occurred, would release, Would instruct
6. we, us, you, your, us
7. conjunction
8. adjective
9. verb
10. noun

REPLAY DRILL 7

1. C
2. F
3. F
4. C
5. C
6. F
7. C
8. F
9. C
10. F
11. F
12. C
13. C
14. F
15. F
16. C
17. C
18. F
19. C
20. F

REPLAY DRILL 8

1. F
2. F
3. C
4. F
5. C
6. F
7. F
8. C
9. F
10. F
11. C
12. F
13. F
14. C
15. F
16. C
17. F
18. F
19. F
20. C

REPLAY DRILL 9

1. C-S
2. C
3. R
4. C
5. R
6. C-S
7. C
8. C
9. C-S
10. R
11. C-S
12. C
13. R
14. C-S
15. C
16. C-S
17. C
18. C-S
19. R
20. C

REPLAY DRILL 10-A

1. therefore
2. for example
3. hence
4. then
5. consequently
6. furthermore
7. otherwise
8. however
9. in fact
10. nevertheless
11. also
12. in addition
13. moreover
14. thus
15. that is
16. for
17. but
18. yet
19. nor
20. or

English for Careers 93

REPLAY DRILL 10-B

1. R
2. C
3. C-S
4. C-S
5. R
6. C
7. C
8. C-S
9. C
10. R
11. C
12. C-S
13. C
14. R
15. C-S
16. C
17. C
18. C
19. C-S
20. C

REPLAY DRILL 11

1. after the workers finished the project
2. until the clouds moved in
3. Because the biscuits were hard
4. Since Susan left town
5. When salesmen are successful
6. Although we had a wet spring
7. even though they have no money
8. when he was president
9. Even though his supervisor gave clear directions
10. Since wrong answers will be subtracted from the total number of correct responses

BONUS DRILL 12

Answers may vary

REPLAY DRILL 13

1. Hebrew Ruth   M E ruth
2. M L assassinus from Arabic hashsháshin
3. F chauvinisme
4. Greek from Homer
5. L fr GR
6. L from GR Tantalus
7. L
8. a la mode F
9. It ciarlatano
10. GR
11. branch of biology dealing with embryos
12. science that deals with history of the earth and its life, esp. rocks
13. scientist who deals with earthquakes and with artificially produced vibrations of the earth
14. any of several elementary particles postulated to come in pairs of similar mass
15. picture script of the ancient Egyptian priesthood
16. concerned with the individual rather than society
17. mental and emotional disorder that affects only part of the personality
18. abnormal fear of being helpless in an embarrassing or unescapable situation
19. the science of human beings
20. statistical characteristics of human populations

REPLAY DRILL 14

1. absence
2. accuracy
3. analyze
4. attendance
5. Britain
6. cemetery
7. changeable
8. changing
9. coming
10. deferred
11. dining
12. excellence
13. existence
14. forty
15. grammar
16. grievous
17. C
18. loneliness
19. ninety
20. omitted

English for Careers   95

REPLAY DRILL 15   DICTIONARY CODES

1. Sep tem ber   3
2. won der ful   3
3. mer ri ment   3
4. meth od ol o gy 5
5. to tal i ty   4
6. noun, verb, adjective
7. noun, verb
8. noun
9. noun
10. noun, verb
11. mod lən
12. e jə kā shən
13. li tə ra chur
14. spas tik
15. bə lūn
16. L
17. M E from M F from L
18. N L from G K
19. L
20. F from O F

BONUS DRILL 16   DICTIONARY REWARDS

1. (Sound Navigation Ranging) method of detecting objects under water by using sound waves
2. (Radio Detecting and Ranging) method of locating and detecting objects by using radio waves
3. (Compact Disk Read Only Memory) a compact disc containing data that can be read by a computer
4. (Videocassette recorder) a videotape recorder that uses videocassettes
5. (Self Contained Underwater Breathing Apparatus) apparatus used to breathe while underwater
6. sensitive to beauty
7. needless repetition of an idea or statement
8. having little substance or strength
9. to weigh in the mind
10. to examine closely
11. to grow by rapid production of new parts
12. to form or move in waves
13. relating to astronomy; enormously large
14. mournful
15. confused
16. GK
17. M E from L
18. F from O F
19. F
20. It

REPLAY DRILL 17

1. babies
2. alloys
3. daisies
4. plays
5. rallies
6. countries
7. churches
8. taxes
9. wishes
10. glasses
11. vetoes
12. echoes
13. radios
14. altos
15. leaves
16. roofs
17. shelves
18. wives
19. chiefs
20. dwarfs

REPLAY DRILL 18-A

1. theses
2. bacteria
3. analyses
4. stimuli
5. algae
6. genera
7. hypotheses
8. curricula/curriculums
9. memoranda/memorandums
10. fungi
11. antennae
12. appendixes/appendices
13. syllabi/syllabuses
14. crises
15. plural
16. singular
17. plural
18. plural
19. plural
20. singular

REPLAY DRILL 18-B

1. S
2. P
3. S
4. P
5. P
6. P
7. S
8. S
9. P
10. S

REPLAY DRILL 19-A

1. Bushes
2. Kellys
3. Joneses
4. Hartmans
5. Jameses
6. Maries
7. Amys
8. Williamses
9. Booths
10. Loises

REPLAY DRILL 19-B

1. get-togethers
2. post offices
3. runners-up
4. cupfuls
5. sons-in-law
6. tapedecks
7. photocopies
8. hand-me-downs
9. middlemen
10. letters of credit
11. German
12. Christmas
13. United Airlines
14. April
15. Commander
16. Personnel Department
17. Statistics
18. Purchasing Agent
19. East Coast
20. President

REPLAY DRILL 20

1. firefighter
2. doctor
3. flight attendant
4. women
5. author
6. photographer
7. new manager
8. director
9. police officer
10. feminists
11. that lawyer
12. mail carrier
13. a secretary
14. clergy
15. synthetic, manufactured, artificial
16. managers and their spouses
17. spokesperson
18. colleague/coworker
19. weatherperson, weathercaster
20. workers

REPLAY DRILL 21

1. irresistible
2. stationery
3. statue
4. receive
5. recommend
6. picnicking
7. i tal yən
8. rän di vū
9. a cər tān
10. mē dē vəl
11. kar bō hī drāts
12. fə rō shəs
13. having originated in, growing or occurring naturally in a particular region
14. acceptance as true or real
15. regional variety of language
16. combination of social and economic factors
17. part of the essence or inmost being
18. a fixed pattern, oversimplified opinion or prejudiced attitude
19. thoroughly overwhelm
20. knowing, perceiving

BONUS DRILL 22

1. media
2. cacti, cactuses
3. attorneys
4. parties
5. deer
6. sheep
7. IRA's
8. children
9. appendices, appendixes
10. bacteria
11. alumnae, alumni
12. teeth
13. algae
14. series
15. species
16. basis
17. lives
18. calves
19. hooves
20. knives

REPLAY DRILL 23

1. I
2. us
3. They
4. me
5. We
6. him
7. they
8. us
9. me
10. He
11. her
12. us
13. she
14. me
15. I
16. me
17. her
18. We
19. us
20. He

REPLAY DRILL 24

1. he
2. she
3. themselves
4. he
5. me
6. he
7. I
8. himself
9. themselves
10. ourselves
11. C
12. <u>myself</u>   I
13. <u>him</u>   he
14. C
15. <u>theirselves</u>   themselves
16. <u>hisself</u>   himself
17. C
18. <u>himself</u>   he
19. C
20. C

REPLAY DRILL 25

1. its
2. whose
3. your
4. No one's
5. yours
6. Who's
7. everyone's
8. They're
9. mine
10. ours
11. It's
12. Who's
13. you're
14. Somebody's
15. yours
16. whose
17. anyone's
18. their
19. My
20. its

REPLAY DRILL 26

1. who
2. who
3. whom
4. whoever
5. who
6. Whom
7. whom
8. who
9. who
10. Who
11. whom
12. whoever
13. who
14. whom
15. whom
16. Whoever
17. who
18. Whomever
19. who
20. whom

REPLAY DRILL 27

1. Every one
2. Someone
3. anybody
4. somebody
5. Any one
6. Everything
7. nobody
8. Everyone
9. Something
10. Anything
11. their
12. her
13. his
14. their
15. his
16. their
17. his or her
18. his or her
19. their
20. their

BONUS DRILL 28

1. its
2. its
3. its
4. their
5. its
6. their
7. their
8. its
9. their
10. its
11 – 20 answers will vary

REPLAY DRILL 29

1. jogs — present
2. should sing — future
3. cries; leaves — present
4. laughed — past
5. is marrying — in progress
6. will fly — future
7. stays — present
8. have been seeing — in progress
9. wanted — past
10. will paint — future
11. is typing — in progress
12. needs — present
13. is looking — in progress
14. marched — past
15. will arrive — future
16. recommended — past
17. gained — past
18. is considering — in progress
19. will talk — future
20. climbs — present

REPLAY DRILL 30

1. taken
2. stands
3. spoken
4. seen
5. ran
6. rose
7. rang
8. gone
9. gave
10. flew
11. eaten
12. drank
13. does
14. chose
15. broken
16. begun
17. worn
18. took
19. rung
20. drunk

REPLAY DRILL 31

1. wrote
2. thrown
3. sang
4. shaken
5. hidden
6. froze
7. forgotten
8. fallen
9. drew
10. come
11. blew
12. bit
13. written
14. threw
15. sung
16. sank
17. shook
18. hit
19. fell
20. drawn

REPLAY DRILL 32

1. Are
2. is
3. were
4. had been
5. are
6. Is
7. are
8. I would
9. will be going
10. will be
11. is
12. are
13. is
14. are
15. were
16. will be
17. have been
18. were
19. have been
20. We would

REPLAY DRILL 33

	SUBJECT	VERB
1.	sun	rose
2.	wolves	howled
3.	you	do have
4.	cooking	is
5.	(you)	answer
6.	newspaper	is delivered
7.	students	are
8.	mother, son	were found
9.	director	sent
10.	you	did buy
11.	restaurant	is
12.	sign-ups	will be held
13.	word	spread
14.	Mr. Overton	attended
15.	manufacturer	recalled
16.	boy, grandfather	strolled
17.	courses	are taught
18.	residents	were warned
19.	Sidney	will learn
20.	team	practiced

REPLAY DRILL 34-A

1. singular
2. plural
3. singular
4. plural
5. singular
6. plural
7. plural
8. singular
9. plural
10. singular
11. plural
12. singular
13. plural
14. plural
15. singular
16. singular
17. plural
18. singular
19. plural
20. plural

REPLAY DRILL 34-B

1. writes
2. want
3. arrive
4. am
5. was
6. does
7. is
8. cries
9. records
10. speak
11. is
12. talks
13. are
14. are
15. tries
16. is
17. is
18. were
19. has
20. does

REPLAY DRILL 35

1. were
2. was
3. was
4. was
5. were
6. were
7. was
8. were
9. were
10. was
11. were
12. was
13. was
14. were
15. were
16. were
17. was
18. were
19. were
20. were

BONUS DRILL 36

1. has
2. spends
3. selects
4. has
5. is
6. greets
7. have
8. votes
9. its
10. scatters
11. shouts
12. approves
13. decides
14. plays
15. pay

REPLAY DRILL 37

1. this
2. these
3. them
4. Here
5. That
6. Those
7. those
8. These
9. these
10. That
11. these
12. this
13. that
14. this
15. those
16. Those
17. This
18. This
19. Those
20. That

REPLAY DRILL 38

1. a
2. an
3. a
4. an
5. an
6. an
7. a
8. a
9. an
10. a
11. a
12. an
13. an
14. a
15. a
16. an
17. a
18. a
19. an
20. a

REPLAY DRILL 39

1. Everybody
2. any
3. can
4. anywhere
5. ever
6. any
7. anything
8. anywhere
9. any
10. ever
11. can
12. ever
13. any
14. any
15. anywhere
16. can
17. any
18. could
19. ever
20. any

REPLAY DRILL 40

1. best
2. kind
3. better
4. pretty
5. friendliest
6. brightest
7. efficient
8. harder
9. faster
10. quick
11. more recent
12. least valuable
13. farther
14. worst
15. less
16. oldest
17. wider
18. most beautiful
19. younger
20. sweetest

REPLAY DRILL 41

1. softly
2. expensive
3. very
4. swift
5. rapidly
6. delicious
7. accurately
8. bad
9. patient
10. beautifully
11. happily
12. busily
13. pretty
14. real
15. really
16. clearly
17. fair
18. sour
19. sure
20. well

REPLAY DRILL 42

1. <u>best</u>   better
2. <u>good</u>   well
3. <u>deliciously</u>   delicious
4. <u>efficienter</u>   efficient
5. <u>more logically</u> logically
6. <u>late</u>   later
7. <u>safely</u>   safe
8. <u>fastly</u>   faster
9. <u>quicker</u>   quickly
10. <u>sourly</u>   sour
11. <u>calmly</u>   calm
12. <u>sure</u>   really
13. <u>wider</u>   more widely
14. <u>smoother</u>   more smoothly
15. <u>better</u>   best
16. <u>handsomely</u>   handsome
17. <u>careful</u>   carefully
18. <u>quiet</u>   quietly
19. <u>swift</u>   swiftly
20. <u>rapid</u>   rapidly

REPLAY DRILL 43

1. child
2. engine
3. customer
4. judge
5. afternoon
6. factories
7. secretaries
8. months
9. children
10. Virginia
11. men
12. company
13. accountants
14. months
15. year
16. women
17. employees
18. European
19. waiter
20. student

REPLAY DRILL 44

1. secretary's
2. men's
3. bosses
4. Booths'
5. repairman's
6. clerks
7. employee's
8. company's
9. freshman's
10. professor's
11. mother-in-law's
12. congresswoman's
13. child's
14. members
15. Williamses
16. actresses
17. tenants'
18. months'
19. directors
20. Today's

BONUS DRILL 45

1. none
2. can't
3. o'clock
4. We'll
5. Don't
6. It's
7. IRA's
8. a's and an's
9. 7's and 11's
10. 50's and 60's
11. C's
12. A's
13. RN's
14. Won't
15. CPA's
16. t's and i's
17. wouldn't
18. 10's
19. '90
20. v's

REPLAY DRILL 46

1. English, accounting, and payroll
2. to be organized, to speak clearly, and to show enthusiasm
3. The company president and the managers and the supervisor
4. Washington, Philadelphia, and New York City
5. child abuse, single-parent families, and homeless shelters
6. The students, their parents, and their teachers
7. The chefs, the cooks, and the waiters
8. shoes, shirts, and long pants
9. main dish, vegetable, and dessert
10. to type, to proofread, and to mail the reports
11. fold, bend, or staple
12. October 5, November 9, and January 15
13. Pineapples, kiwis, and mangos
14. rent, phone bill, and electric bill
15. her meats at Super Fresh, her produce at Farm Fresh, and her grocery items at Food Lion
16. parents, agent, and director
17. swimming, boating, and snorkeling
18. the streets, the alleys, and the buildings
19. The surgeon, the lab technician, and the radiologist
20. her birthday, her anniversary, and her daughter's wedding.

REPLAY DRILL 47

1. hot, humid
2. old, battered
3. chocolate, chewy
4. two eggs, one stick of butter, and two cups of flour
5. bright, cheery
6. warm, gentle
7. hard, crunchy
8. intelligent, competent
9. ketchup, mustard, and relish
10. accurate, efficient
11. long, fierce
12. friendly, honest
13. to run, to jump, and to dance
14. to dust the furniture, to peel the potatoes, and to iron the shirts
15. daring, competent
16. ridiculous, comic
17. hot, salty
18. a rose, a $100 gift certificate, and a big smile
19. operating system, accounting procedures, and auditing methods
20. skinned his knee, bruised his arm, and broke his front tooth.

REPLAY DRILL 48

1. , and
2. , and
3. , but
4. , yet
5. , but
6. , and
7. , but
8. , nor
9. , for
10. the shoes, the purse, or the hat
11. , but
12. , and
13. , yet
14. , but
15. , for
16. , nor
17. , and
18. , yet
19. , and
20. , for

REPLAY DRILL 49

1. Yes,
2. Mrs. Smithers,
3. dawn,
4. begins,
5. No,
6. arrive,
7. Bryant,
8. work,
9. stopped,
10. reunion,
11. outside,
12. Well,
13. school,
14. door,
15. Oh,
16. work,
17. Olivas,
18. door,
19. mall,
20. do,

REPLAY DRILL 50

1. , who likes to surf,
2. , Mr. Harvey,
3. , Toni Heiser,
4. , *Guide to Business Careers*,
5. , young or old,
6. , who is my brother-in-law,
7. , Mr. Pope?
8. , Mr. Orton,
9. , *Understanding Business Mathematics*,
10. , yes, or no,
11. , who is also a dentist,
12. , my favorite baseball team,
13. , Mr. Hunting?
14. , Janet Sturn,
15. , Mrs. Norfleet,
16. , *Wings*?
17. , ladies and gentlemen,
18. , who is also my aunt,
19. , Mr. Breeden,
20. , Dr. Morgan?

REPLAY DRILL 51

1. Norfolk, Virginia,
2. Washington, D.C.,
3. Madrid, Spain,
4. June 12, 1975,
5. , James Kail, D.D.S.,
6. August 25, 1991,
7. San Francisco, California,
8. Anaheim, California, Orlando, Florida?
9. , Ph.D.,
10. , September 6, 1974.
11. Portsmouth, New Hampshire, Portsmouth, Virginia?
12. , M.D.,
13. , October 14, 1989,
14. Tampa, Florida, Charleston, South Carolina?
15. Thursday, September 5, 1991.
16. November 15, 1989,
17. , Ph.D., M.D.,
18. Richmond, Virginia, Montreal, Canada.
19. Monday, October 5, Wednesday, October 12.
20. , M.D., Longport, Rhode Island

REPLAY DRILL 52

1. Friday?
2. C
3. C
4. "Please,"
5. "Watch out!"
6. C
7. C
8. C
9. instructed,
10. C
11. C
12. C
13. yelled "Goodbye"
14. week?"
15. C
16. C
17. Marvin asked,
18. C
19. C
20. C

English for Careers 115

REPLAY DRILL 53-A

1. , not
2. , not
3. very, very
4. , never
5. C
6. sunny, sunny
7. , never
8. , seldom
9. walk, walk
10. , never
11. , not
12. speak, speak
13. , not
14. , not three
15. , never
16. , not
17. , but
18. , seldom
19. , not
20. , never

REPLAY DRILL 53-B

1. 516 Belmont Avenue, Chicago, Illinois
2. C
3. , but
4. June 13, 1991
5. Yes,
6. , Mrs. Tieg,
7. office,
8. C
9. in the sandbox, splashed in the kiddie pool, and
10. fast, accurate
11. educated, yet
12. , of course,
13. vice president, George Hampton,
14. Boston, Massachusetts, Charlotte, North Carolina?
15. company, you
16. C
17. Mr. Williams,
18. records, and
19. September 1, not
20. C

REPLAY DRILL 54

1. period
2. exclamation mark
3. period
4. question mark
5. exclamation mark
6. period
7. period
8. question mark
9. exclamation mark
10. period
11. question mark
12. period
13. exclamation mark
14. exclamation mark
15. period
16. period
17. period
18. period
19. exclamation mark
20. question mark

REPLAY DRILL 55

1. meeting; and
2. bus; then
3. accident; therefore,
4. could; nevertheless,
5. raise; that is,
6. job; then
7. council; the
8. town; and
9. months; hence
10. years; therefore,
11. hits; still
12. jobs; also
13. bonds; thus
14. early; yet
15. Massachusetts; Portsmouth, New Hampshire; and Augusta, Maine
16. raise; however,
17. course; nevertheless,
18. birthday; his
19. contract; therefore,
20. arguing; thus

English for Careers 117

REPLAY DRILL 56

1. utensils:
2. 5:45
3. Karen's goals were:
4. mind:
5. Gentlemen: Ladies and Gentlemen:
6. C
7. 8:30   11:45
8. thing:
9. United Parcel:
10. Council:
11. highest:
12. holidays:
13. 11:30
14. class:
15. C
16. diet:
17. specials:
18. interviews:
19. Opening:
20. 8:00   8:30

REPLAY DRILL 57

1. "accept"   "except"
2. "I can"   "I can't"
3. "Thank you, Mr. Lockner,"
4. C
5. yelled, "We're lost!"
6. entitled "Uses for Quotation Marks"
7. "What time will your plane arrive?"
8. "Employee of the Year"
9. cheered, "We won!"
10. "eligible"   "illegible"?
11. "Money Management"
12. "break a leg."
13. "ain't"
14. asked, "Are you working overtime tonight?"
15. "Don't Feed Me!"
16. "Les Miserables"
17. wondered, "Should I order dessert?"
18. "irregardless"
19. yelled, "Play ball!"
20. "catch a wave"

Student Prep Book—Answers

REPLAY DRILL 58

1. up-to-date
2. first-rate
3. C
4. self-respect
5. out-of-stock
6. four-year
7. ten-story
8. hard-to-find
9. part-time
10. high-priced
11. ninety-nine
12. mid-July
13. self-control
14. well-dressed
15. six-foot
16. brother-in-law's
17. kindhearted
18. high-risk
19. third-class
20. self-respect

REPLAY DRILL 59

1. weeks'
2. Mr. Hernandez'
3. children's
4. child's
5. boss's
6. secretaries'
7. someone's
8. Janice's
9. woman's
10. ladies'
11. Franklin's
12. James's
13. authors'
14. mother-in-law's
15. months'
16. employees'
17. Minister's
18. companies'
19. Joneses'
20. teachers'

BONUS DRILL 60

1. (believe me)
2. (not now)
3. (not $59)
4. (9 to noon)
5. (see Figure 4, page 80)
6. (last year's models)
7. (our first minister)
8. (not her sister)
9. (see chart, page 23)
10. (the one near the mall)
11. donation—we
12. Happiness—it's
13. money—a
14. refrigerator—rated number one by Consumer Reports—has
15. supervisor—a real sweetheart—
16. members—Dr. Duzeck and Ms. Swenson—will
17. Crack—thousands
18. beauty—the
19. Sharmita—she was the winner—praised
20. computer—the color printer is included—is

REPLAY DRILL 61

1. F
2. I
3. B
4. G
5. D
6. H
7. A
8. J
9. E
10. D

REPLAY DRILL 62

1. C
2. G
3. D
4. I
5. A
6. F
7. B
8. H
9. E
10. J

REPLAY DRILL 63

1. F
2. C
3. G
4. E
5. A
6. B
7. I
8. H
9. J
10. D

REPLAY DRILL 64

1. D
2. G
3. H
4. C
5. K
6. E
7. B
8. L
9. A
10. I

REPLAY DRILL 65

1. G
2. C
3. L
4. E
5. H
6. B
7. I
8. D
9. K
10. J

English for Careers

BONUS DRILL 66

1. C
2. A
3. C
4. A
5. B
6. C
7. A
8. B
9. A
10. C
11. B
12. A
13. A
14. B
15. B
16. B
17. A
18. B
19. B
20. B

REPLAY DRILL 67

1. course
2. physical
3. bizarre
4. except
5. elicit
6. counsel
7. Air
8. hear
9. descent
10. dye
11. cite
12. capital
13. alter
14. effect
15. excess
16. coarse
17. fiscal
18. accept
19. illicit
20. council

REPLAY DRILL 68

1. waive
2. roll
3. principal
4. peace
5. naval
6. led
7. its
8. minor
9. past
10. pare
11. raze
12. stationary
13. peddle
14. residence
15. waste
16. You're
17. principles
18. stationery
19. passed
20. residents

REPLAY DRILL 69

1. adapt
2. adept
3. regardless
4. humane
5. envelop
6. imminent
7. advise
8. beside
9. choose
10. bibliography
11. desert
12. devise
13. defer
14. eligible
15. conscience
16. adopt
17. chose
18. eminent
19. differ
20. advice

REPLAY DRILL 70

1. than
2. reality
3. perspective
4. lose
5. personal
6. suite
7. quite
8. proceed
9. prosecute
10. weather
11. thorough
12. were
13. prerequisite
14. respectfully
15. moral
16. realty
17. quiet
18. personnel
19. precede
20. persecute

REPLAY DRILL 71

	ERROR	CORRECT
1.	off of	from
2.	should of	should have
3.	off of	off
4.	among	between
5.	waiting on	waiting for
6.	I	me
7.	must of	must have
8.	near to	near
9.	going to	going
10.	she	her
11.	I	me
12.	could of	could have
13.	between	among
14.	off of	from
15.	might of	might have
16.	I	me
17.	off	from
18.	should of	should have
19.	off of	from
20.	may of	may have

BONUS DRILL 72

1. A
2. A
3. B
4. B
5. A
6. B
7. B
8. B
9. A
10. B

REPLAY DRILL 73

1. Having taken too many sick days,
2. C
3. Biting quickly on the bait,
4. C
5. C
6. Torn around the edges,
7. Sitting on the windowsill,
8. C
9. C
10. Having received good grades,
11. Being on the discount table,
12. C
13. C
14. Feeling as though she was in labor,
15. Jogging quickly around the block,
16. C
17. Before going home,
18. C
19. After browsing through the store,
20. C

REPLAY DRILL 74

1. Allen majored in the executive secretary program at business school.
2. Chris plays football on the junior varsity team.
3. There was a good sale at the store at the mall.
4. The juicy hamburger was covered with onions.
5. The loud ticking gave Marissa a headache.
6. After he completed his homework, he had a snack.
7. While reading the comics, Brenda laughed.
8. Kenneth decided to go on a diet since he weighs 183 pounds.
9. Linda and Freddie split a large popcorn at the movies.
10. Classes will begin on Crystal's birthday, September 3.

	VAGUE PRONOUN	CORRECTION
11.	she	Elley
12.	They	The IRS
13.	they	her friends
14.	her	Helen's or Patricia's
15.	he	Mark or Frank
16.	You	Students
17.	she	Leslie
18.	it	running
19.	You	Patrons or Customers
20.	he	Lance

REPLAY DRILL 75

1. some hay
2. with the beautiful voice
3. with the crack in the middle
4. with the chocolate swirls
5. with two flat tires
6. with the speed bumps
7. with the furry tail
8. with one textbook
9. with the thorns
10. which was misplaced this morning
11. NP
12. C
13. C
14. NP
15. NP
16. C
17. C
18. NP
19. NP
20. NP

REPLAY DRILL 76

1. D
2. I
3. D
4. I
5. D
6. D
7. I
8. D
9. D
10. I
11. D
12. I
13. D
14. D
15. D
16. I
17. I
18. D
19. I
20. D

BONUS DRILL 77

Answers will vary

REPLAY DRILL 78 – 80

1. T
2. F
3. T
4. F
5. F
6. T
7. T
8. F
9. T
10. F
11. T
12. T
13. F
14. F
15. F
16. T
17. F
18. T
19. F
20. F

BONUS DRILL 81

Answers will vary